Sow Your Seed

CULTIVATING LIFE'S JOURNEY FOR HARVEST

Midohoabasi Essienubong

NEW HARBOR PRESS

Rapid City, SD

Essienubong/New Harbor Press
1601 Mt. Rushmore Rd, Ste 3288
Rapid City, SD 57701
www.NewHarborPress.com

Sow Your Seed / Midohoabasi Essienubong. —1st ed.
ISBN 978-1-63357-325-3

To my late mother, Mrs. ImeObong Essienubong, who practically taught me that my life is a valuable seed and whose foresight prepared me for every stage of life.

To every young person and indeed everyone seeking to harness the seeds and resources God has deposited in them.

Contents

FOREWORD

IT IS A RARE honour and a great privilege for me as the biological father of this budding author to pen the foreword to his book debut. MidohoAbasi is from a family that loves the Lord. He was brought up in the tradition of prayer and deep study of the Word. I recall that during family devotions, everybody brought to the table profound insights to all Bible discussions. I can't forget in a hurry how my late wife, whom he has paid glowing tributes to in this work, used to enrich such discourse with her in-depth analysis. So, MD, as he is fondly called, grew up to love the Lord and surrendered his life to Christ at a very early age. Even while in High School, he was a pride to the family. On his school *Open Days* for instance, parents and guardians had the opportunity to interact with each subject teacher as they moved with their wards from stand to stand. Such days were always very revealing to parents as they usually heard directly from their wards' subject teachers. While many of my son's mates earned a spank or more from their disappointed parents for their misdeeds, MD on the other hand received accolades from his teachers without exception. They always spoke of him in superlatives.

It is not surprising, therefore, that his seminal work had to originate from the seed of regular devotion planted in him by the family and further boosted by The Holy Spirit as he continued in that habit of regular devotion. This work which is presented in seven chapters is premised on the fact that **"everything we have in life today started in a seed-like form".** Thus the author encourages us to sow whatever seeds we are endowed with without any hesitation. But to do that, we have to take a cue from the agricultural farmer who prepares the soil, plants the seeds, and protects them from weeds/thorns while reckoning on God's sovereignty to give him a bountiful harvest. In his assertion, **"...the concept and principles of farming are timeless, there is so much we can learn from them in the pursuit of our purpose on earth"** because as he rightly puts it "**man is inherently a farmer and human life is basically a seed**".

The book which unfolds chronologically provides answers to such fundamental questions of life as: **"who am I?"** and **"why am I here?"** It so well informs us that we are in this planet to play a role no one has ever played or will ever play. Thus the book opines that our roles in life which are basically for God enable Him to reach others through us as well as reach us through others. We are reminded to reflect on the fact that problems that exist in our lives and in the society at large are potential seeds that must be cultivated. Thus the author maintains that in every life there is a seed to solve human problems. So, as observed earlier, the book takes us through all the stages of farming starting from the need to cultivate the soil as all soils are not appropriate for all crops. And for an eventual bumper harvest, the seeds do not only need roots to grow, they need good weather and protecting from all possible enemies. As an ardent believer in the sovereignty of God, the author impresses upon us the fact that all our efforts notwithstanding, increase or growth comes from God; and it is God's desire that at the end of the day, we should enjoy the fruits of our labour and return all praises to Him.

The small but fascinating book is laced with the author's personal experiences in a lucid exposition on Christ's *Parable of the Sower* as recorded by Apostle Mark. There are many well-articulated eye-catching statements by the author and quotations/aphorisms from other sources in the book that will appeal to readers of all ages. For instance, the author asserts and it is axiomatic that **"hard work is needed to be successful and hard work is required to remain successful"**. The inspirational book which is unapologetically predicated on Christ's teaching, is a must read for young people of all faith especially those who do not want to come to this world in vain. The older generation will have a lot, of course, to glean from it as well. I, therefore, with all sense of responsibility, enthusiastically recommend this book to all and sundry. I assure you, this treasure in your hands will arrest your attention once you pick it up to read and you may find it difficult to discontinue until you are done with it. It has blessed my life; it will bless yours as well. Happy reading!

—Okohanienkpoh Essienubong
(PASTOR / MARRIAGE & RELATIONSHIP COUNSELLOR)

ACKNOWLEDGEMENTS

This work is a result of the contributions and cooperation of great minds and wonderful people who inspire and motivate me to fulfill God's will, plan and purpose for my life. I feel a deep sense of gratitude to:

My beloved parents, Pastor Okohanienkpoh Essienubong and Mrs. Amina Essienubong, for their unwavering support. Special thanks to my father for editing the manuscript and for the invaluable suggestions which were instrumental in bringing this work to life.

My irreplaceable siblings, Mrs. Stanley UtengeAbasi, Eduek, Abasibiangake and Abasiama who are my unapologetic cheerleaders. I love you all.

Stephanie Thomas, for believing in me, patiently listening to me, responding to my unending emails, and never getting tired of the lengthy meetings. Your contributions to this work cannot be quantified.

The RCCG friends and family in Europe Mainland, Pastor Zion Okuneye and Pastor Edmund Emmanuel of the RCCG family in Poland. I'm humbled by your words of encouragement, endorsements and prayers.

Finally – God the Father, the Son, and the Holy Spirit; the one I live for. Who works in me and through me to live a life worthy of the call He has designed for my destiny.

INTRODUCTION

WHEN THE WORD 'SEED' is used in the Christendom today, it is most times associated with giving. As a result, many have become uneasy at the mention of the word in the church or wherever believers gather. You may have heard a phrase like: "if you have been blessed today, sow a seed to God in appreciation". Many Christians understand the concept of 'seed' today only from this narrow perspective. We forget that everything we have in life today started in a seed-like form.

This book looks at the concept of seeding from an entirely different perspective. There is so much to learn from seeds both in planting and in harvesting. Life as it were mirrors the concept of sowing and reaping. In this book, therefore, we try to look at seeds and what we do with them as a parallel to our lives. In other words, we can apply to our lives the principles of cultivating seeds and reaping harvests.

The central message of this book is developed from the teaching of Jesus in Mark 4: 1-9 known as *the parable of the sower*. The teaching of Christ from this parable is primarily about the kingdom of God, the word of God, salvation and receiving of the gospel. This work does not attempt to re-write the message of Jesus Christ from that parable. Rather, like every other message from the Scriptures, the lessons from this parable can be applied to our lives in various ways. What I am aiming at is to share with you some of the lessons I learnt while studying this parable at a time in my life when I needed a redirection and reorientation. I must confess that I did not initially set out to turn the lessons so learned into a book. But during one of my morning devotions at some other time, the Holy Spirit began to teach me fresh lessons from this same parable. As I wrote down those few lessons (which eventually turned out not to be few), I came to believe that those lessons were not meant for me alone but for as many as I could possibly share them with, especially young adults who are battling everything life is throwing at them.

There has never been a time in history such as now when young people are confused, pressured and dissatisfied with life. I am not saying I have cracked the code or that I have all the answers to life's puzzles, but I am saying that the word of God is more than enough to help everyone out there to redirect his or her life's journey and find fulfillment in cultivating the seeds God has deposited in him.

All through the Holy Scriptures, we see parables associated with planting and agriculture. This is no surprise because one of the first commands God gave to man was **"...Be fruitful and multiply and replenish the earth, and subdue it"** (Genesis 1: 28). God put Adam in the Garden of Eden to tend and till the ground. In other words, man's first major assignment was to cultivate the land. This shows that sowing and reaping has been with man since creation. In today's world, farming is often despised and hardly regarded as a 'noble profession' whereas in the beginning, man hardly had any other source of survival. The passage of time notwithstanding, human beings still depend so much on farming; both subsistence and mechanised for sustenance. Unfortunately, as vital as farmers are to the society, they are not often given the recognition and the credit they deserve. For instance, in Nigeria where I grew up, I observed that farmers were seriously undervalued, especially the small scale or subsistent ones. Initially, I thought that was only peculiar to that environment. But having lived in other countries, I have equally seen farmers given little or no recognition. With technological advancements in agriculture, I fear that generations may come that may not appreciate the primitive farming skills and the dedication of early farmers who perhaps had nothing except hoe, seedlings and sometimes a hard and uncooperative soil and weather to deal with. They had to contend with everything including pests, observing the seasons, improving seedlings, studying the soil, the risks and health hazards that went with it and so much more. Most of them learned farming practices informally through trial and error and/or the mentorship of their parents and other farmers within their communities. With research and formal education, agricultural studies have improved such that natural resources and elements which are beyond man's control like the sunlight, weather conditions, etc. vital to the growth of food crops can now be simulated and somewhat controlled or regulated to maximize yields. This is why we now have seasonal food and cash crops being grown in and out of their natural seasons. We are in a dispensation where big corporate farmers maximize resources to engineer techniques, robots and automated machines that do all the challenging farm work. We are in an era whereby mobile applications can be used to help farmers achieve better yields. This is not to suggest that farming today is no longer challenging; it is. That is why we should appreciate the dedication, passion, patience, commitment and discipline of our forebears in cultivating the land before the advent of mechanisation and digitalised agricultural processing. Those basic farming skills, techniques and disciplines were passed down from generation to generation, until industrialization and urbanization happened and people abandoned farming for more attractive white-collar and pink-collar jobs.

Because the concept and principles of farming are timeless, there is so much we can learn from them in the pursuit of our purpose on earth. I believe man is inherently a farmer and human life is basically a seed. Perhaps if we take a closer look at our lives the way farmers look at seeds or seedlings, we would make better use of our time on earth. I must emphasise at this point that our daily living is a continuous, conscious and unconscious sowing and reaping. How we live daily determines the nature of our harvest.

As years go by, one begins to discover that one's plans, priorities, thoughts, location, physique, etc. do change. Amidst these changes, the seeds God deposited in us from the day we were conceived in our mothers' wombs remain constant and become even more pronounced as we grow and seek ways to harness and express them. Therefore, discovering the seeds God has deposited in us is the primary step towards engaging and harnessing them. For us to discover our seeds, we must first understand that God created us for a purpose. We are not on this earth for head count, but we are here to count. We are not here by mistake but we are here to have a stake in what happens here. We are not here as spectators but to run a race and make our mark. We are here to be active participants in the affairs of life. We are here to give to the world what only we can give.

My beloved, let me remind you of the fact that no one who has ever lived before you and no one will ever be born who will play the role meant for you on earth better than you are supposed to play. If you occupy your mind with this, you would have set yourself on the path to self-discovery. You hold the answers to so many unanswered questions and unsolved puzzles in this world. You would have cheated the world if no one benefits from your seed in the ultimate. It must be your daily desire and prayer to affect lives positively with the seeds in you. You were created in the image and likeness of God (Genesis 1: 26). You are a 'god' with a small 'g' (Psalm 82:

6). You possess the attributes of God who is your Father. You have the ability to create and bring into existence whatever you visualize or dream.

God's first work was to solve a problem. The earth was formless, empty and dark, then God said, **"let there be light"** (Genesis 1: 1 - 3). Man, therefore having been made in the image and likeness of God has the capacity to identify problems and seek solutions to them because basically, we are here to solve problems. God could have created a perfect world where there would be no problems to solve but rather He decided to deposit seeds in man to enable him (man) solve problems. The proof that we were created in the image and likeness of God is our instinct to solve problems and our ability to create things on the earth. All the creativity we see in the world today is God's power at work in man. When you look at the birds of the air, the beasts of the field, the creatures in the waters, plants and other natural phenomena, we see the beauty, the creativity and the Excellency of God. Over the centuries, man has employed all available resources to explore and exploit the works of God's hand and yet has not been able to complete it. More explorations, organisms, inventions, etc. are still being unravelled. This is a clue and a pointer to the enormous ability and creativity man possesses from God. With the unlimited abilities we possess, it is rather sad that many of us would leave the earth without exploring the potentials in us. God will not do for us what he has given us the power and the authority to do. We have a responsibility to dig deep into the word of God to discover the power we have and assume our godlike roles on earth or live and die like mere men.

After God created the animals and birds, they were nameless. That indeed was a problem. But because God had deposited in man the seed to solve problems, He presented the creatures to man to name them. Whatever names man gave them have been their names ever since. So, the first problem man solved was to give God's creatures names. God identified another problem; man had no helper that was suitable for him. All the creatures named by man put together, none was good enough to be a helper to man. God caused a deep sleep on man and created a woman from him. This means all along, the solution to man's loneliness was embedded in him. Man was carrying the seed of woman within him all this while; a seed he would desperately need. This is evidence that we all carry the seeds to the solutions we seek. The questions you should therefore ask yourself are: Do I know my seed(s)? Am I ready to cultivate them?

I trust God that this book will give you the needed insight into how and why you should look at your life like a seed that needs to be cultivated. I see you being guided towards making good use of what God has deposited in you to better your life and your world and glorify God in the ultimate.

CHAPTER 1

IN SEARCH OF A SEED

ELEMENTARY BIOLOGY TEACHES US that a seed is the unit of reproduction of a flowering plant capable of developing into another plant of its kind. Everything that is important in life begins like a seed. All seeds are unique due to the capabilities and potentials inherent in them. Every living thing has one form of seed or the other. In you, for instance, are the seeds of your progenitors. That's why you sound like them, act like them and look like them. This is essentially why life on earth is a continuum.

In addition to reproducing themselves, seeds also provide edible fruits and leaves. Through the seed God has deposited in you, you have what it takes to reproduce your kind biologically and otherwise. This is the reason some specific abilities and skills are well pronounced in people from a certain linage, origin or geography and absent in others. These are seeds that have been passed down from one generation to the other.

#Your life is your seed.

God in His infinite wisdom has given you some unique abilities. These abilities make you important to your environment in particular and to the world at large. To discover your seeds, you must ask yourself two fundamental questions:
1. Who am I?
2. Why am I here?

Your inability to answer these fundamental questions about your life will keep you loafing through life. Consequently, you would be confused in your life and may never find your bearing all through life. It is not in the power of anyone to determine how long he wants to live on earth. So, the more time you waste wandering through life, the less chance you have to grow your seeds and experience the harvests God expects from you.

Who am I?
Jesus spent thirty-three years on earth in what many consider a short life. The truth however is that He knew who He was and started cultivating His seeds from the age of twelve.

> **"Why were you searching for me?" he asked. "Didn't you know I had to be in my Father's house?"**
> **-Luke 2: 49 (NIV)**

At twelve, Jesus recognised He was not just the son of Joseph but the Son of God. This knowledge set Him on the path to maximizing and cultivating the seeds in Him. Until a person understands who he is, life would just happen to him. So, understanding your origin is an important key to understanding and knowing who you are.

> **Then God said, "Let us make mankind in our image, in our likeness, so that they may rule over the fish in the sea and the birds in the sky, over the livestock and all the wild animals, and over all the creatures that move along the ground." Genesis 1:26 (NIV)**

You were made in the image and likeness of God. This is a pointer to who you are. An image is the representation of an external form of a person or thing. Therefore, you are the external form of God whom you represent. As you seek to understand God and base your choices and decisions in life on Him, the knowledge of who you are will further receive a boost. The Holy Bible has more than enough descriptions and explanations of who God is. It gives us valuable knowledge about God through the help of the Holy Spirit. So, if you do not study the Holy Scriptures, how do you expect to know God? And if you do not know God, how do you expect to know who you are? If you do not know the power of God, how can you express and exercise the power He has given to you? Let me tell you my dear, the Christian Bible is the best resource for self-discovery. This has been my personal experience and testimony.

I recall in my high school days as a boarding student, we had worship service every Sunday led by some Christian teachers who took special interest in our spiritual growth (God bless them and their offspring wherever they are now). There was a particular Sunday worship service that featured a guest speaker which I cannot forget in a hurry. We generally looked forward to having guest ministers because they never had personal experiences and interactions with us students.

So, they never tailored their sermons to address specific vices and atrocities we indulged in as students unlike our teachers who knew us very well and preached what we considered 'judgemental' sermons. The guest minister looked at one of us in the congregation and asked: "who are you?" The student quickly answered giving his name, class and age. The guest minister quickly added "I did not ask you to tell me about yourself, I asked who you are". At that point, there was a pin drop silence in the hall. Never in my life had I given thought to this question. The more I thought about the question, the more I couldn't find an answer. For the first time in my life, it looked like I had never really defined or understood my life; I felt like I had no identity. I cannot recall all that was said in the sermon that day but I remember leaving the worship service with a resolve in my heart to dig deep into the Holy Bible to find out who I am. That was the beginning of the unravelling of my life. The more I studied to know, the more I began to see myself as outlined in the Holy Scripture and not what people made me believe I am.

Many times, our opinion of who we are is based on what we have been told we are. Never let the opinion of anyone define you. There is no way you'll diligently study the Holy Bible to discover yourself that you won't end up discovering who God is to your life and what He says about your life. A song writer wrote and I quote:

I know who God says I am
What He says I am
Where He says I'm at
I know who I am

Seek to know what is written about you in the Word of God and hold on to them. Confess, meditate and walk in the path of what is written about you. Let the Word of God define you.

Why am I here?
I am always reminded of this question when I hear the news of someone's death. Why would anyone come to this world and leave with absolutely nothing to show for it? I mean, what's the point of this life? When I heard my mother had gone to be with the Lord, I kept asking myself why she had to leave the world at the time she did. Prior to this, I had never lost anyone so dear to me. It later dawned on me that life is indeed temporal. While mourning her loss, I searched my soul for the reason of existence on earth. This gave me a deep sense of why God chose her to be my mother for twenty-five years and to be part of my family. The reason God allowed her to be part of my upbringing became clear to me. She had a

role to play in my life and she stayed on course to the end. Searching for answers to the reason she came to this earth gave me a sense of fulfilment and peace about her exit and I appreciated her role in my life more after her death. This further spurred me into finding out the reason I am on this earth.

We all have different roles to play on earth and we should not shy away from assuming those roles. When you leave this earth, will people feel your impact on their lives? Have you ever asked yourself: "what would I like to be remembered for?" Your ability to understand and answer the question of why you exist will keep you on your toes always. God brought every one of us to this world for a reason. You are here for a purpose and that purpose is not in your place to choose or de-termine but God's.

Dr. Myles Munroe of blessed memory said: **"when the purpose of a thing is unknown, abuse is inevitable"**. When you do not know why you are on earth, you are bound to abuse your life. Abusing your life simply means abnormal use (ab-use) of your life and abnormal use of your life means living contrary to God's plan for you. Jesus Christ is a perfect example of someone who knew why He was on earth.

> "You are a king, then!" said Pilate. Jesus answered, "You say that I am a king. In fact, the reason I was born and came into the world is to testify to the truth. Everyone on the side of truth listens to me." - John 18: 37 (NIV)

Jesus made it clear that He came to this world to testify of the truth. He was absolutely sure He came as a proof of God's love for mankind. Why are you here? Irrespective of how you were born or the circumstances surrounding your birth, you are not on earth by error; you are here by divine orchestration. The channels (your biological parents) through which God chose to bring you into this world has nothing to do with the reason you are here.

You are here for God's Pleasure
First understand you are here because it pleases God to bring and keep you here at this point in time. God is in heaven and He does whatever pleases Him (Psalm 115: 3). It pleases Him for you to exist now on the earth and that is why you are here. Even as children of God, there are many things we do because it just pleases us to do them. Pleasure is simply a happy feeling of satisfaction

and enjoyment we could derive from anything or from nothing.

I recall when I was studying on the Island of Cyprus; I loved to sit out by the side of the Mediterranean Sea during the summer in the cool of the evening. I loved the view of the sea, the calmness of the water, the wind and the waves that sometimes blew across the place. It was always a wonderful sight to behold. I did this a lot of times for the fact that it gave me pleasure to be there. The scene always reminded me of the greatness of God. Just as we have pleasure in doing some things, in the same vein, it gives God pleasure to keep us here.

> **God saw all that he had made, and it was very good. And there was evening, and there was morning--the sixth day.**
> **—Genesis 1: 31 (NIV)**

God saw the works of His hands that they were very good and He acknowledged it. I can imagine God smiling and nodding His head in satisfaction for a job well done, and that's you! You are part of that job, you bring Him pleasure and that's why you are here.

**Thou art worthy, O Lord, to re-
ceive glory and honour and
power: for thou hast created all
things, and for thy pleasure they
are and were created - Revelations 4: 11(KJV)**

Have you ever successfully executed a project and whenever you look back at it you become
pleased? There's an unexplainable feeling of pleasure and fulfilment that come with doing something well by yourself. You should make your life
to be pleasing to God by consciously living for
Him daily. Many of us are more concerned with
pleasing man rather than pleasing God. We go
to any length to please our bosses, spouses and
friends at the expense of God. Many see God as
a solution dispensing machine; always wanting
from God but never asking themselves if their
lives are pleasing to Him. They seek God when
they need solutions to their problems. They look
at His hand and not His face. Even when He answers their prayers in His mercy, they make no
attempt to look at His face. Listen to what Jesus
said of the Father when He was here.

**The one who sent me is with me;
he has not left me alone, for I al-**

ways do what pleases him. -John 8: 29 (NIV)

Can you confidently say your deeds are pleasing to God? Have you allowed your flesh get in the way of pleasing Him? Can God look on you and say: "this is my beloved son or daughter in whom I am well pleased"? Remember you are here to please God. If you discover your life doesn't please Him, it is time to reconsider your decisions and amend your ways.

You are here to worship Him.
By nature, we are worshippers. Worship is the feeling or expression of reverence and adoration that's appropriate to God. Worship is our heart finding solace and rest in God on a continuous basis. It's a zone where nothing else matters but God. It's a state where we are willing to cast everything we own and everything we have acquired before God's throne.

> The twenty-four elders fall down before him who sits on the throne and worship him who lives for ever and ever. They lay their crowns before the throne and say:[11] "You are worthy, our Lord and God, to receive glory

and honour and power, for you created all things, and by your will they were created and have their being. -Revelations 4: 10 – 11 (NIV)

When we talk of worship, we sometimes think it is a slow tempo spiritual song we sing in the church. No, worship is much more than that. Signing spiritual songs is not worship but an expression of worship. We can express our worship to God in diverse ways: signing, dancing, prostrating, kneeling, raising of hands, reading out His word, etc. Worship is bringing ourselves to a point of acknowledging the sovereignty and the power of God and the fact that we can do nothing without Him. Therefore, true worship of God should be reflected in our daily living and not just in the church or wherever we gather for worship. Worship is yielding ourselves totally to God and turning over our wills and thoughts to Him. It is casting down our crowns and bowing our hearts in humble adoration to Him. It is total submission to God borne out of love for Him and not by compulsion or as a routine. Essentially, therefore, worship is God centred. We are sometimes told to worship Him so He can bless us and answer our prayers but we forget we are to worship Him because of who He is. The moment your worship of God is based on your expectation, it's no longer true worship. The reason many can't worship God especially when their prayers are yet to be answered is because the worship of many is predicated on what they can get from Him. Worship is not external but internal; it begins from the heart. No wonder, God is interested in our hearts (Proverbs 23: 26). When Samuel went to the house of Jesse to anoint a king, here is what God said:

> **But the LORD said to Samuel, "Do not consider his appearance or his height, for I have rejected him. The LORD does not look at the things people look at. People look at the outward appearance, but the LORD looks at the heart."**
> **1st Samuel 16: 7 (NIV)**

The conversation of Jesus with the woman at the well in John 4: 19-24, highlights the true meaning and mode of worship. First, Jesus made it clear that worship has nothing to do with geographical location, legislation or custom. The coming of Jesus Christ gave everyone, both the Jews and the Gentiles unhindered access to God. It was no longer a matter of location, but a matter of relation.

The knowledge of God is also very central to our worship. Jesus said to her: **"you worship what you do not know"**. A personal relationship with God increases our knowledge of Him. If you do not have a personal relationship with Him, the bare truth is that you do not know Him. The woman at the well was born to see her fathers worship the way they did but she had no understanding of who they worshipped. Some of the deepest descriptions of God I have heard from believers always erupt during true and spontaneous worship. When you love someone and you have a personal relationship with him, you would naturally interact with him in a special way. You would give him some unique names that befit his status. From the words we utter during worship, it is easy to tell our conviction and our revelation of God. Most times, men catch a revelation of God in the place of true worship. The beautiful thing about having a personal relationship with God is that your knowledge and experiences in fellowship with Him will increase just the way you know people better through personal interaction. Worship makes you realise you will never come to a point where you can say you know all of Him or have seen all of Him rather you would always thirst for more of Him. This will further impact on your understanding and mode of worship. The more you grow in the knowledge of Him, the more you seek ways to express and reverence Him.

#True worship comes only from spirits made alive and sensitive by the quickening of the Spirit of God - John Piper

We cannot worship God the way we choose but the way He chooses. God seeks worshippers who will worship Him in Spirit and in Truth. God is a Spirit and our spirit is the core of our being. So, our worship must transcend the physical to be impactful. Worshipping in the spirit means engaging our hearts and minds totally. It means being under the influence and total control of the Holy Spirit. Worshipping in truth means being properly informed and having adequate knowledge of who we worship. Truth here is translated from the Greek word 'aletheia' which means 'true' and is derived from the word 'alethes' which means 'to take notice'. God expects us to 'take notice' of the truth about Him. He doesn't just need your worship but He deserves it because you were created to worship Him.

You are here for service
Jane moved into a new neighbourhood and observed how her visually impaired octogenarian neighbour struggled once every week to shop at

the grocery store. The aged woman always went shopping with her dog, her only companion. The steep path to the grocery store never made the journey easy and she had tripped over the pavement a couple of times sustaining minor injuries. Jane had a busy schedule as a nursing assistant but always had a heart to serve. It was for this reason she decided to train as a nursing assistant after so much struggle coming from a non-privileged background. Jane took it upon herself to ask her neighbour what she needed weekly and endeavoured to go shopping for her. She went further to use her spare time in helping the neighbour do some cleaning. Jane made her aged neighbour's life more interesting than it was before she started helping. The story of Jane sums up service in a very simple but impactful manner. Service is making another person's life better.

Many think of service in different ways depending on so many factors. Some people from the developed world think of service as volunteering in an orphanage or in some disadvantaged villages somewhere in a third world country. Sometimes, it's a skewed logic propagated in some quarters to drive home a certain narrative. This is good but it's just a little fraction of what service to humanity entails. Service is much more than all of that; it is realizing that your life on earth is to make another person (your neighbour) more fruitful and productive.

Irene lost two family members within one and a half years. As if that was not enough, she lost her job also and for a long time, none was in sight. Added to that, she was trusting God for a life partner. It was a very trying time of her life; so she had many challenges to worry about. In the midst of all that, she heard of a woman who died during child birth leaving behind a beautiful baby girl at a nearby local hospital. The father of the baby was jobless and incapable of nursing the baby. The father approached nurses in the hospital to hand over the baby for adoption but no one was willing to adopt the baby. Irene believed the baby should not be denied the care of a mother and decided to adopt the baby. Although she had nothing to survive on, she trusted God to take care of her and the baby.

Not quite long, some people who heard of her kind heartedness started trooping in with both financial and material gifts for her and the baby. Through the magnanimity of the public, her needs were met while the baby experienced motherly love and care. It is a truism that when you make yourself available for the good of others, God will raise tools and resources that will enable you to carry out that desire with ease. So for her kind gesture, God blessed her with more than enough.

#Service is making another man's life better

God is always pleased with us when we take up the responsibilities expected of us. Taking care of the needs of others is service to God. You cannot love God without loving those He created in His image. The purpose of service is for God to reach others through our lives and for God to reach us through other people. You can't imagine how many people God would reach through you if you yield yourself totally to Him. What greater way can we express our love to God than making ourselves available to serve those He loves? When we put the needs of others before us, we are indeed making a sacrifice and rightly directing the attention of others to God. When we serve others, it helps us tame the flesh which is selfish and self-centred. Serving others brings out the best in us. We realise our true self by not responding to the selfish demands of our flesh. To find yourself, you must first lose yourself in service to others.

This service that you perform is not only supplying the needs of the Lord's people but is also

overflowing in many expressions of thanks to God.[13] Because of the service by which you have proved yourselves, others will praise God for the obedience that accompanies your confession of the gospel of Christ, and for your generosity in sharing with them and with everyone else. - 2nd Corinthians 9:12-13 (NIV)

Your service to humanity brings praises to God. It puts testimonies and praises in the mouth of others. Wouldn't it be satisfying to know that your act of service is the reason people affirm their trust and believe in God? Each day, you should think of how you can improve the well-being of others. If you are waiting to meet all your needs before you improve the well-being of others, you will live and die without impacting any life positively. Just like the story of Jane and Irene, they had their own struggles, it wasn't all rosy with them yet they understood they were in a better position to make other lives better.

A story was told of a father and son who saw a fish struggling to survive at the bank of the sea. The waves of the sea had pushed the fish to the sea bank. The father took the fish and put it back into the water and the son asked, "dad what difference does it make, there are thousands of fishes in the sea?" The father replied, "it makes a lot of difference to the fish we have just saved that was outside the water and struggling to survive". Look out for the little things that could mean a lot to a life out there. If it means a lot to just one person, it is worth doing. We are sometimes engulfed and preoccupied with our daily struggles and the quest to live better and happier lives, running from north to south and east to west like headless chickens, dying slowly with little or no fulfilment. We ignore our neighbours who may be 'bleeding to death' blaming our lack of compassion on lack of time because of doing 'service to God' or 'working for God' like the Priest and the Levite in Luke 10: 30 - 37 who passed by a dying man after an encounter with bandits. The Priest must probably have been on 'an urgent assignment' or 'mission' for God thus being 'too busy' to attend to any other thing including a dying man.

#Are you too busy to attend to a dying soul?

We are sometimes too busy pursuing mundane things while ignoring the things that matter and the very essence of our presence on earth. So many things around us cry for our help and seek our attention. We can begin by asking people around us simple questions such as "How can I help you?; Do you need any help?" Many people around us appear invisible because we can see everything else but their pain. Taking notice of someone else's pain even if you can't offer any tangible help may be enough to give him the strength and the hope for living. The world today has defined goals for us which may be fair but not necessarily good for everyone. If you are not careful, you could live your life trying to meet these targets that may not add value and meaning to anyone's life. The world could engage you in multiple of ways so as to prevent you from cultivating the seeds in you. Hear what the Holy Spirit said to the Corinthian church through Apostle Paul.

> **"I have the right to do anything,"
> you say—but not everything is
> beneficial. "I have the right to do
> anything"—but I will not be mas-
> tered by anything. – 1st Corinthi-
> ans 6: 12 (NIV)**

You might have the right to pursue certain goals and dreams but are they expedient? Do they contribute to why God brought you here? Do they contribute towards making another man's life better? Are they what is needed?

To serve, you must be able to identify what is good and what is needed. Recall the story in Luke 10: 38 - 42 when Jesus visited Mary and Martha. Mary sat at the feet of Jesus listening to Him teach. Martha was busy trying to fix a meal for Jesus. Martha wanted to make Jesus as comfortable as possible and this was culturally and humanly the right thing to do. Martha complained to Jesus that Mary ought to help with the preparation of the meal but hear what Jesus said to Martha:

> "Martha, Martha," the Lord answered, "you are worried and upset about many things,[42] but few things are needed - or indeed only one. Mary has chosen what is better, and it will not be taken away from her."
> —Luke 10: 41 - 42 (NIV)

Probably, Mary considered it a rare privilege to listen to Jesus teach the Scriptures in private and she needed to listen to Him with undivided attention. In the same vein, there are some services you need to jettison irrespective of people's opinion. There is always something that is worth being considered above every other thing.

*#To serve, you must be able to differenti-
ate what is good from what is needed.*

God's desire is that His children lookout for
each other's need. Jesus was asked what the greatest law is and He said inter alia:

> **"'Love the Lord your God with all
> your heart and with all your soul
> and with all your mind.' This is
> the first and greatest command-
> ment. And the second is like it:
> 'LOVE YOUR NEIGHBOUR AS
> YOURSELF'"** (BOLD mine) -
> Matthew 22: 37 - 39 (NIV)

Having love for your neighbour will open your
eyes to the ways and the opportunities at your
disposal to serve them. A wise person will always
pray for opportunities to serve because it is also
a window to express and reaffirm one's love for
God. The driving force for service is love, if you
can't love, you can't serve. 1st Corinthians 13: 4
- 8 says that love is patient, love is kind. It does
not envy, it does not boast, it is not proud. It does
not dishonour others, it is not self-seeking, it is
not easily angered, it keeps no record of wrongs.
Love does not delight in evil but rejoices with the
truth. It always protects, always trusts, always

hopes, always perseveres. When you examine each characteristic of love from this passage, you would discover that these are the same yardstick or template for service. Love and service are inseparable. In service, you don't live for yourself but for others.

The Bible says of King David:

> **For David, after he had served his own generation by the will of God, fell asleep, was buried with his fathers, and saw corruption - Acts 13: 36 (NKJV)**

David is a good example of someone who served his generation by the **will of God**. It is God's will for every man to serve. David served as a king having been anointed of God in that capacity. Today, many people hardly understand the position they occupy as a privilege to serve God and humanity. The world would have been a better place if leaders in government and in the private sector realised that the position they occupy is for them to better the lives of others and not to amass wealth for themselves at the expense of those they serve. Apostle Peter wrote:

> **Each of you should use whatever gift you have received to serve**

others, as faithful stewards of
God's grace in its various forms.
1st Peter 4: 10 (NIV)

We all have something that we can use to
serve. There's no man on earth that is deficient,
poor or lacking in gifts from God to serve the
body of Christ, his neighbours, community, environment and the world. There is nothing we have
that doesn't come from God (John 3: 27) while
all good and perfect gift are from above (James
1: 17). We all have various measures of grace be-
stowed upon us to serve and divine gifts are not
for selfish purposes. Freely have we been given
and freely should we use in serving others. We
are enjoined not just to serve but to do so faith-
fully. Our service is continuous, having no expi-
ration date till we depart this world. Our gifts are
different both in purpose and in quantity even
when they appear similar.

As long as the earth endures, seedtime
and harvest, cold and heat, summer and
winter, day and night will never cease.
—Genesis 8: 22 (NIV)

As long as there is life sowing and reaping must
continue. In fact, life is about sowing and reaping
as earlier indicated. Sowing is the only process

by which seeds can be multiplied. The mystery of sowing, all things being equal, is in the harvest which is always more than the seed sown. Your life today is a function of what you have always cultivated. It is often said that "when preparation meets with opportunity, success is inevitable". Just as in an ideal situation, only the qualified for a job opening will have a shot at such an opportunity. Your success in life will to a large extent be hinged on how prepared you are to make good use of what I call 'success vacancies' when they beckon. How much and how well you have sown will also reflect on how far you can go with every 'success vacancy' that knocks on your door.

#Seeds are not all meant to be eaten, some are meant to be sown

I believe there's always an opportunity, no matter how insignificant or slim they may appear for every man to succeed or take a giant leap in different areas of life. I understand life doesn't offer the same opportunities to everyone, sometimes we may have to 'create' the opportunities for ourselves. The major problem most times however is lack of preparation or inability to recognise them when they show up. For some, when opportunity comes in a way they did not expect, they don't make use of it. Your ability to identify and utilise opportunities that can usher in success and growth is what will make you stand out from the crowd. The man who is not interested in potato farming wouldn't recognize the season to plant potatoes and would not keep track of the time to harvest them. You need to have interest to sow and a hunger to succeed at it. This is what would make you to know why you sow, what you sow, when to sow and more importantly, how to sow. If you sow nothing, you will harvest nothing. In other words, your failure to sow means you are sowing something which is nothing and you'll harvest something which is nothing.

#You cannot harvest what you did not sow.

It is also important to know that you may never find the right time or the opportunity to sow your seed. A lot of people sometimes get fixated on the right time to sow. Take hold of every opening, launch out and sow your seed. Some of us spend too much time looking for the best opportunity to launch out for that evangelism, that business, that trade, to make that phone call, to record that song, to write and publish that book or to embark on that trip. Don't wait until the situation is perfect in your own eye, it may never be. The Preacher says:

Whoever watches the wind will not plant; whoever looks at the clouds will not reap.[5] As you do not know the path of the wind or how the body is formed in a mother's womb, so you cannot understand the work of God, the Maker of all things.[6] Sow your seed in the morning, and at evening let your hands not be idle for you do not know which will succeed whether this or that, or whether both will do equally well - Ecclesiastes 11: 4 - 6(NIV)

Many times, people make statements along the lines of, "I am waiting for the right time to start it." This is not to downplay the importance of doing what is right at the right time, you have less challenging hurdles when you do what is right at the appropriate time but it should not stop or restrain you from sowing when you can. As a matter of fact, when you closely examine statements such as "I am waiting for the right time to do it", you'll discover they emanate from one form of fear or the other. Procrastination most times is a child of laziness. Just launch out and sow your seed now because 'the right time' of your mind may never come.

#*You may never find the right time to sow, do it now!*

A farmer who plants potatoes has a glimpse of the harvest he expects both in quantity and in quality. The challenge many of us face is that we fail to sow when we should therefore; it is difficult to catch a glimpse of the future. For others, they just love to imagine without taking any steps. These are wishful thinkers and no action backs up their imagination. Their thoughts are simple wishes or phantasmagorical. Acting on your thoughts and dreams is the only route to bringing them to reality. Your dreams are at best wishes until they manifest.

#*Sowing equips you for the future.*

Many commit their lives to the hands of fate; some leave theirs in the hands of people while some take charge of theirs. Always learn to be at the driver's seat of your life. The good news about being the driver is that you would be conditioned to learn the route. You will assume a sense of responsibility because you know you have a role to play towards the success of the journey. There is always a reawakening sense of responsibility when you take charge of your life choices and decisions. Take responsibility for your actions and become accountable for them. When you become passive about matters that concern you, it gives room for you to blame others for your failure. No one would give you a seat in the bus of destiny until they are comfortably seated, so why don't you aim at becoming the driver?

#No matter how full a bus is, there is always a seat for the driver. Be the driver!

No matter how much damage you feel people have caused you, you can always make repairs. No matter how long people have delayed your dreams from manifesting, you can always push further by taking decisive actions. No matter how much damage people have done to your dreams, you can always dream again. No one can stop you from daring to dream, it costs absolutely nothing to dream. Never participate in a game where your victory is dependent on the motivation, actions or inactions of others. For instance, one of the ratings of a football coach is dependent on the repeated success that is achieved when his players execute his tactical instructions, game plan and game play. No matter how good a coach is, if his players decide to go against his instruction and fail to execute his instructions, the coach would be deemed to have failed. Sometimes, football managers are one poor game away from losing their job. I understand it might be difficult or even impossible to avoid situations where your progress is devoid of human influence but as much as possible, always try to oversee your own game, dictate it. Take responsibility for your life, your failures and shortcomings, this is the first step to recognizing, accepting and owning your seed which is your life. I am not in any way suggesting you should be hard on yourself, I am only saying you should mentally put yourself in a better position to fight back and walk through challenges that oppose your seed sowing mission. Do away with the 'entitlement mentality' otherwise, it would keep you stagnant and stranded. In pursuit of your dreams, always act as if no one owes you anything. I am not suggesting that people do not owe you anything but because human beings are fundamentally flawed and you have to be more proactive when dealing with people because man will always fail you. Let your life be shaped by decisions you made and not by decisions you did not make or by decisions others made for you.

#Take responsibility for your decisions, leave the blame game.

There is always a lesson to be learned from every situation. Learn the lesson, accept responsibility for the part you played in it and move on.

When you fail to learn the lesson, opportunities will always rise where you need to learn them again. Sometimes, you might need to admit you created or helped fuel the problem in the first place. This is not to infer that no one may have been directly or indirectly responsible for whatever unfavourable or undesirable position you find yourself today but perhaps you were complicit. Whether rightly or wrongly, when you blame others for your challenges you would inadvertently be giving them power over you. You are invariably saying 'he is the one in charge of my life' or 'she is the reason I'm still at this spot'. That way, people would dictate your feelings and your emotions. Have you forgotten your heavenly father rules in the affairs of men, including your life? Why allocate so much power to other men over issues concerning your own life? This is one reason I do not subscribe to the school of thought that credits everything wrong to the devil. This is not to say that the devil does no wrong, there are many wrongs he does (Matthew 13: 25). But fixing your gaze on him and his actions doesn't bring any solution either. "O devil, you spilled the milk, my only cup of milk. Why did you do it, why? Now I'll be hungry for the rest of today. O devil you are really evil, now my room is messed up...." but you haven't cleaned the mess or gone in search of fresh milk. Can you see the problem?

Okay, the devil did it so what's next? Are we going to sit here and mourn forever? We sometimes take this kind of attitude to God in our prayers, rather than pray and make our request we spend time complaining to God about the problem without seeking the solution and His help. Just like the man by the pool of Bethesda (John 5: 1 - 9), Jesus asked him a very simple question "Do you want to get well?" A simple 'Yes' would have been enough but he began explaining the problem; "I have no one to help me into the pool when the water is stirred. While I am trying to get in, someone else goes down ahead of me..." He had no idea he could receive his healing instantly without going into the pool. He had no clue the man talking to him could heal him without the pool. He thought his problem was the process of getting into the pool when all he needed was access to the healer who was right before him. When you pray, make sure your prayer doesn't stem from the position of fear of the devil but of reference for the All-knowing and Sovereign God. There's an expression I used to hear from my father which says: **"Don't tell God how big your problem is, tell the problem how big your God is".** When you take your eyes off the problem and the devil or whoever is to be blamed for your current challenges, your mind will be rightly positioned to focus on correcting and finding a lasting solution. And maybe if you looked closer, embedded in your problem might be the very same seeds your destiny needs to come alive.

> **#Every problem has in it the seeds of its own solution. If you don't have any problems, you don't have any seeds - Norman Vincent Peale**

As you go in search of a seed and for the meaning to your life, see the problems that exist in your life and in society at large as potential seeds that need cultivation.

CHAPTER 2

LAUNCH OUT WITH A PURPOSE

Again Jesus began to teach by the lake. The crowd that gathered around him was so large that he got into a boat and sat in it out on the lake, while all the people were along the shore at the water's edge. 2 He taught them many things by parables, and in his teaching said: 3 "Listen! A FARMER WENT OUT TO SOW HIS SEED. (BOLD mine) Mark 4:1-3 (NIV)

LIFE IS A SEED and until you realize the reason you have it, you may never know what to do with it. It is one thing to have seeds, it is another thing to go out there and cultivate them. The farmer according to the parable in Mark Chapter 4 did not launch out for just any reason; he went out to SOW his SEED. That was his purpose. He took his first step, he launched out. A popular saying goes thus: "the journey of a thousand miles begins with a step". It is usually exciting to see a baby take his first steps to walk. It might be frustrating to him at the onset. But with repeated attempts, he gets stronger and begins to gain balance. Before long, he does not only walk confidently, he begins to run around even to the point that restraining him becomes difficult.

What it means to launch out isn't different from the experience of that baby. At some point in our lives, we just have to take that first, bold and sometimes fragile and awkward move or step if we want to sow the seeds we possess. The act of sowing requires movement, requires launching out, requires exploring and may also require seeking information. Man's life is not a standby power generating set; it should be mobile with a purpose. In junior high school, we were taught an acronym **'MR. NIGER D'** which helped us to easily recall the characteristics of living things. The first letter 'M' stands for 'Movement'. Movement characterises life. If you are not making meaningful advancement, you are literally dead. Even after you have taken that first step and it seems like nothing is working, take it again. In Luke 5: 1 - 7; Simon, a professional fisherman and his colleagues had toiled all night for fish yet caught nothing. They had taken all the needed steps to catch fish but were not successful. They washed their nets and were about retiring for the day. One can imagine their frustration. While in that state, Jesus instructed Simon: "...launch out into the deep, and let down your nets for a catch". Simon replied; "Master, I have worked through the night without catching anything..." Simon had legitimate reasons to have believed that launching out again was a bad idea and was likely to be a fiasco. He was experienced enough to think that taking another step would be an exercise in futility. However, he obeyed and this time he was successful. The lesson here is simple, dig deeper! Take that step again; you might get another insight or another perspective on it. You might make a useful observation that hitherto eluded you or you might even get the answers or the solution you could not arrive at earlier. Like Simon, many times we are prone to making excuses as to why we shouldn't launch out again or why we shouldn't cast our nets a second time. At some other times, we may be simply tired and worn out because of human nature. Irrespective of how weak you are or how plausible your excuses are, your seeds are too precious for you to ignore. Launch out a second time or even a third time.

Learn to assess different areas of your life from time to time: areas where you are stagnant, where you have not made any significant progress and improve upon them. It is better to move at a snail speed than to be stagnant. So many people complain bitterly about how life treats them but they never launch out or take that first step; some have never launched out to sow any seed God has deposited in them.

Expand your social circle
Launching out could also mean expanding your circle of friends and community. By nature, we gravitate towards people who are most like ourselves hence we create social circles with people whom we share similar backgrounds and life experiences. They include people who look like us, talk like us and behave like us. It is within such companies that one feels comfortable. Launching out could also mean connecting with people that are fundamentally different from you in their approach to life. I don't mean engaging people who don't share your values. You shouldn't engage with people on some certain levels if your core values are divergent. However, expanding your

social circle to include people that contrast you in their outlook to life could be very challenging yet very meaningful and useful. Expand your network to include people that are of a different race, ethnic group or with different political orientation and ideology from yours. You will learn valuable lessons that only this kind of interaction can teach. If for instance, you work with a team of people who always see things the same way you see things, such a team may never achieve any remarkable feat in the pursuit of a common goal because there is no alternative thinking, no one is thinking out of the box. Once in a while, there should be someone that goes against the grain not in an antagonistic fashion or for the sake of an alternative opinion but in an effort for the best. For instance, my understanding of evangelism, witnessing and outreach expanded when I began interacting with people who have a burning desire for evangelism and have the call of God on their lives for that ministry. They could see an avenue for evangelism right under my nose that I could not see. Relationships such as these are beneficial not just to our physical and intellectual growth and development but also to our spiritual growth and walk with God. Have you ever wondered why we are all one in the body of Christ but we are different parts? In 1st Corinthians 12, Paul talks about the various gifts in the body of Christ using an analogy of the various parts of our body. Like parts of the body, all these parts have different functions but they all work in synergy. This analogy can be applicable to our daily living. There is so much to learn from interacting with people different from us. God can use the experiences of people different from you to teach you lessons. The missing link in your life might just be found if you expand your social circle to accommodate diverse opinions, thoughts and dreams which could give more leverage to your launching out and seed sowing mission.

Explore new ideas
Launching out could also mean exploring new ideas, taking a new job, increasing your capacity, learning a trade or enrolling for a degree, doing something new, doing something different and doing something more. Remember the popular saying: "ideas rule the world". Never get tired of seeking new ideas and seeking new opportunities. Never get tired of discovering new routes and do not be afraid of stretching beyond your perceived limits, no one can limit you. We all have that point we believe is our limit but if we push further, we may discover we can go beyond that artificial limit we set for ourselves. We have unlimited abilities because at the end, we are the ones creating limits for ourselves. For many, this

only exists in the realm of their perception but not in reality for we can do all things through Christ who strengthens us (Philippians 4: 13). When you launch out, it means you are open to new ideas and you are willing to let go some principles, values and cultural systems or beliefs that are counterproductive to your seeds and subsequently your harvest. Launching out could mean viewing the world from the lens of others, breaking away from unprofitable relationships, making new friends and business or career partners. Until you launch out with a purpose, you will never appreciate the world outside you. There are people ready to work with you and help you groom your seed but how will they cross your path if you never launch out or if you never interact with people. You cannot make any meaningful progress if you do not meaningfully interact with people. Human beings are the greatest resource on the planet and no man is an island. A proverb in my mother tongue says: **"a poor man is not someone who has no food; a poor man is someone who has nobody"**. What this age long proverb elucidates is the fact that it is more valuable to have people around you than material riches. When you have people who are concerned about you, you stand a better chance of winning the battle against financial or material poverty. In trying to cultivate your seed, you will discover the usefulness

57

of people God has placed around you and people that cross your path.

I once met a businessman who said to me one of the ways he conceives new business ideas is to travel to different places, meet new people and see how things are being done there. He would pack his bag and visit a new place for a week or two, it might be in another state, country or continent to observe the environment and the people. He said he makes this kind of trip once every year because it inspires new ideas in him. There are challenges some societies have conquered but other societies somewhere are still grappling with because they haven't gone out to seek solution. Launching out can be an inspirational and motivating force to seek ways to harness your seed. Launching out helps you appreciate the challenges that exist out there and can trigger a hunger in you to proffer solutions to them. Launching out opens your eyes to the world around you. Launching out could mean seeking knowledge about the reality of others. The world has become so synergised and globalised that from the comfort of your room, you can have adequate information about a place or a people. If you are conditioned to only one environment, chances are that you will never learn anything new or you will learn new things at a very slow pace when the world has moved on from them. This may give you a close-minded approach to life. Launching out could mean seeking new, uncommon and creative avenues to express your gifts and potentials.

Man – an important resource
We all come from the union of two people and we all affect the lives of other people in various ways than we fail to admit as we are also impacted and influenced by the lives of others. Like the African proverb that says; **"it takes a village to raise a child"**, your life today is influenced by most of the people you grew under. Man is therefore an important resource in the seed sowing enterprise of other men. Sometimes you need just one person that believes in your seed to boost your confidence in launching out. The stories of greatness of many are always linked to the lives and influence of other men. Men are used in deciding the promotion or demotion of other men. I learned quickly at work that vital work-related decisions about me will always be taken when I am not in the decision room. What men perceive you to be will inform the decisions they make about you in your absence. God uses men to bless other men, and when you find favour with God you will find favour with men. Jesus found favour first with God and then with man (Luke 2: 52).

Let's briefly look at how the people (specifically women) God placed in the life of Moses were instrumental to him living his purpose and growing his seed. The story of Moses recorded in the Holy Scriptures has so many twists and turns from his birth to his death. Moses was a great leader of God's people and a very typical example of one who fulfilled purpose in spite of opposition. Moses started fighting the battles of life from birth. The greater your purpose, the greater your battles are likely to be. Finding and living your purpose come with battles you must overcome. A careful study of the life of Moses reveals he achieved all he did partly because, at every low point in his life, there were people around him God used to lift and encourage him. The more I study the life of Moses, the more I realise I shouldn't take the people God has placed around me for granted. I have learned to be grateful to God for them and I have also learned to be careful of who I allow to impact or influence me.

Shiphrah and Puah (Exodus 1: 15 - 21)

Shiphrah and Puah were Hebrew midwives who disobeyed King Pharaoh's order to kill new born Hebrew boys because they feared God. Their decision made it possible for Moses to be alive. They risked all to please God because they feared Him more than they feared their Egyptian authoritarian leadership. Not to forget that Egypt was the most powerful nation on earth at the time. In other words, King Pharaoh was powerful and feared both at home and aboard. The penalty for going against his orders was death but God spared the midwives. I am sure they had no idea that their action to disobey the King would mark the beginning of Israel's freedom. So, even before Moses was born, God had raised and positioned people He would use to spare His life from the hand of a murderous King. In the same token, before you were conceived in your mother's womb, God had positioned people that would be instrumental to His plan for your life. Some people have been strategically positioned by God to cross your path at certain points in your seed sowing programme just to make sure your harvest is secure.

Whenever I go through this story, my heart is always grateful to the midwives or doctor(s) that assisted my mother in my delivery. I don't know them but I'm grateful to God for their lives. You might think, but "they were only doing their job" but you know, people make mistakes that cost lives while doing their jobs. The fact that I'm here means they did a good job, so it is not out of place to be grateful to them and to thank God for their lives. God has also positioned you to be instrumental to the growth and harvest of other people's seeds. The story of Shiphrah and Puah ended with God giving them their own families.

There is always a blessing attached to making yourself a useful resource to the lives of people.

Jochebed (Exodus 2: 1 - 3)
Jochebed was the mother of Moses. She gave birth to Moses when an order went out from the king that all newly born Hebrew boys must not be allowed to live. You can imagine her apprehension having a baby boy at such trying times!

Her name is mentioned only twice in the Bible; but the little we know about her teaches us a lot about the kind of mother she was. Jochebed was able to discern that something was special about her baby. There are mothers like her who see the uniqueness in their children. For three months, Jochebed successfully hid baby Moses from the blood thirsty agents of the king. I cannot say how she did it; I have been in a home with babies few times and I know how hard it is to make them keep quiet. When there's a new baby in a neighbourhood, everyone there will know. They sometimes cry at odd times especially at night and it could be very devastating caring for them, more so secretly. It was remarkable and courageous that Jochebed could hide him for three months without arousing any suspicion, but it obviously wasn't sustainable. She had to look for a more sustainable means of preserving the baby and she took a greater risk putting the baby in a basket and keeping him at the bank of the river. I am sure she had thought about the possibility of anything going wrong before going on with this plan. She must have weighed the pros and the cons of the decision she was about to make. The baby could be attacked by animals or insects. The love of a mother would go to any length even if it means taking risks and making sacrifices that could offer a chance for the baby's survival no matter how slim that chance might seem. If Jochebed was unable to preserve Moses, it is obvious that he would have gone the way of other children. But God who sent him for a purpose, placed him in the hands of a mother who was able to take the risk to preserve his life. It is no surprise we revere mothers in our world. Motherhood is a blessing to mankind. This story also reminds me to be appreciative of my mother for everything she went through to give me a better chance at life and fulfilling my purpose.

Pharaoh's Daughter (Exodus 2: 5 - 10)
The daughter of Pharaoh went to the River Nile to have a bath and there she saw baby Moses. She had compassion on the baby and decided to adopt him even though she knew he was a Hebrew boy. It is not out of place to assume that this gesture by Pharaoh's daughter was a risky one. While there was an order from the seat of power to kill

Hebrew baby boys, heaven had orchestrated plans for a Hebrew boy to be raised from that same seat of power. Pharaoh's daughter must have had challenges convincing the royal family and the palace community to accept her decision to raise a Hebrew boy within the palace. But when God is involved in a matter, He'll always make a way where there seems to be no way. God strategically positioned Pharaoh's daughter to cross paths with baby Moses who needed all the care and protection in the world.

Miriam (Exodus 2: 4 - 8)

Miriam was the elder sister of Moses. She stood by the bank of the river where his mother had left baby Moses and watched over him. She was brave enough to approach the maids of Pharaoh's daughter and offered to find a Hebrew nurse for the baby. The nurse who was called in to nurse him was no other person than his biological mother. Miriam was that caring, protective and courageous elder sibling Moses needed. Some of us can look back at our lives and see the roles our siblings played in our upbringing and outlook to life. Later in the ministry of Moses, we see how she led the women of Israel to sing victory songs after God had delivered them from the hands of the Egyptians (Exodus 15: 20 - 21). She was named as one of the seven major prophetesses of

Israel. She played an important role in the destiny of Moses and a huge support in his seed sowing journey. A stable and supportive family is a blessing to all the family members. It is not surprising, therefore, that people from a stable family stand a better chance of succeeding in life. Sometimes that extra push or support your destiny needs might come from your parents or your siblings. Learn to be a support system to the family members God has given to you.

Zipporah (Exodus 4: 24 - 26)

You cannot talk about the women that God used in shaping the life of Moses without talking about his wife. At some point, God called Moses to go deliver the children of Israel from the Egyptian bondage. Essentially, God was goading him to launch out into his assignment. Moses left his father-in-law's house with his family on a journey to Egypt. On their way, they lodged somewhere to pass the night and God tried to kill Moses. This is where Zipporah stepped in and circumcised her son and touched Moses feet with the skin. This action by Zipporah spared the life of Moses. There are many commentaries and schools of thought as to why God sought to kill Moses. There may not be any consensus as to why God wanted to take the life of Moses. What is important is that Zipporah knew what to do to save the husband's life at the nick of time. Sometimes in our most vulnerable moments we need people around us that know what to do and know how to intercede to help us get back on our feet. In every sense, Zipporah was a factor in Moses' life to preserve him to fulfil his purpose.

Fear not but Trust God
One reason many do not launch out to sow their seed is fear. Fear of the unknown, fear of what the future holds, fear of failure, fear of what people think or might think of them. Conquering fear is fundamental to launching out with a purpose. Fear from past betrayal have prevented some from being open to people. They miss out on people who could open them to opportunities that might be instrumental to the growth of their seed. Some have become paranoid that they trust no one, not even themselves. I recall listening to a TEDx talk by Cobhams Asuquo, one of Nigeria's foremost multi award winning music producer and songwriter. Blind from birth, he said blind-ness taught him how to trust even when he had no reason to trust. He referenced a childhood story where his elder brother taught him how to jump over open street gutters. Whenever he went out with friends and he was informed of an ap-proaching street gutter, he jumped without ask-ing any questions. Soon enough, he discovered his

friends always told him to jump even when there were no open gutters just so they could have a good laugh. He said even after he found out they played pranks on him, he continued to jump when he was told to jump because staying out of open sewage gutters was more important to him. He still chose to trust regardless of the pranks they played on him. Sometimes you may have to trust even when it makes no sense to trust. Thinking about his life experience, it suddenly dawned on me that for him to live optimally in a world designed for sighted people he had to keep trusting people around him. You can't live life thinking everyone that crosses your path is out to harm or take advantage of you. You must learn to trust people. You can't live life being suspicious of every fly. Living your life with your guard always up is simply living in bondage. Launching out to the unknown requires trust in the people God has planted in your life and it means absolutely trusting God without fear.

#Trust has no expiration date
– Cobhams Asuquo

In Genesis 12: 1, God commanded Abraham to leave his father's house to a place He called "a land I will show you". Abraham obeyed and trusted God to fully take charge of the journey. Many times, we might need to make a move without full knowledge of what the destination entails. My walk with God has always been in this format. I never fully grasp what is ahead; I just follow and wait for His direction and leading. If you can't trust God to lead you even when it doesn't make sense, then you are not ready to make progress in different areas of your life. The evidence of your faith in God reflects in how much you can depend and trust in Him. As humans we always want to figure out everything. The consequence is that you may encounter situations that could make you afraid and you may be tempted to give up. Another aftermath of trying to figure out every-thing is that you may unconsciously begin to seek your own solutions and ways. You may eliminate God from the picture because of fear, forgetting He is the one that brought you to that point in the first place. I love this hymn by Ira Stanphill which always reminds me of where my focus should be.

> **Many things about tomorrow**
> **I don't seem to understand**
> **But I know who holds tomorrow**
> **And I know who holds my hand**

Stop trying to figure out tomorrow but rather focus on the one who knows tomorrow and trust Him to be with you as you launch out with a purpose today. The four lepers in 2nd Kings 7: 3 - 16 understood that if they remained at the entrance of the city gate, they were bound to die either by hunger or by the hands of the Syrians soldiers. So they decided to take chance and go into the camp of the Syrian army not minding what could possibly befall them. They conquered fear! On arrival at the camp of the Syrian army, there was no one in sight but there were plenty of food. After taking care of themselves, they went back to the city to tell the people of their discovery. Their bold step of faith did not only save them of hunger but saved others as well. You do not know how many lives would be touched and saved if you could just conquer fear. Take that bold step of faith and launch out today for you do not know how many generations would be impacted by your purpose. Don't wait until your situation is dire before you launch out to seek for way out. Some people wait until the eleventh hour when all available channels to harness their seeds have almost been closed. Bad situations should spur people to discovering and harnessing their seeds. But why wait for things to really get bad? For instance, does it make sense to wait until you spend your last cent before you search for a job or find ways to earn an income? The problem with the eleventh-hour rush is that you might become too desperate and desperation hardly give room for sound reasoning. Even in prayers, when you pray in desperation, you may have answers to your prayers but your ears may not be open to hear God. Fear feeds desperation and desperation could becloud your sense of judgement.

> *#Find your dreams before your dreams find you. "Dig your well before you become thirsty" - Seth Godin*

A Lesson from the Eagle

The eagle is a unique bird we can learn from especially in the way it trains its young ones. When the mother eagle wants to teach the eaglet to launch out and fly, she first stirs up the nest making it uncomfortable for the eaglets (Deuteronomy 32: 11 - 12). Many people are very comfortable where they are. They fail to launch out because they have been conditioned and restricted to a certain place or level of comfort. They are always afraid of change. One way to kill your seed is to be comfortable where you are forgetting that there is always room for improvement; forgetting there is always room to raise the bar higher. The mother eagle stirs the nest when the eaglet has grown and become too big to stay in the nest. For some of us, God might have to stir our nest and make us uncomfortable before we launch out. Maybe the problem you are currently going through is God stirring your nest because He wants you to launch out for a greater height. He wants you to flex your wings, to fly above the storm. If you must be what God wants you to be, if you must sow your seeds, you have to get out of your nest. You have to realise how small and limited your nest is. You cannot sow inside it, you have to sow outside it, it has to be outside your comfort zone. The seeds God has deposited in you are too big to be restricted to your small nest. How can you flex your wings if you are always comfortable in your nest? How do you know you can fly if you are always in your nest?

I love watching the high jump and pole vault events during the Olympic games. They keep raising the bar until each athlete reaches his limit. Even if you have scaled heights every other athlete in your category failed to scale, the bar keeps being raised for you until you reach heights you cannot scale any more. It is then you can set your best personal record or even break an existing one. This is the kind of mindset you should possess; a mind to always do better than what you have done and to keep lifting the bar for yourself. Even when you are ahead of everyone, don't relax, set a novel record. There's a huge difference between being comfortable and being contented. You can be contented with where you are now but still be yearning and striving for greater heights.

Your hunger for harvests from your seeds must not cease. For instance, hunger for food is a recurring feeling, even if you are satisfied today; you'll be hungry again tomorrow. If you don't have appetite for food, it becomes a problem. Be hungry to see your seeds grow, be hungry to use what God has deposited in you to bless lives and be hungry to find purpose. It's time to stop celebrating the successes of yesterday but rather to explore the possibilities of tomorrow.

#Leave your nest!

Another lesson from the eagle is its excellent vision and concentration. The eyes of the eagle are very powerful, having about 3.6 times human acuity. This powerful sight of the eagle allows it to spot a prey on ground 3.2 km away. This gives it advantage over its prey and competitors (Job 39:27-30). Launching out makes you see beyond your immediate environment because what you see is what you will have. If you want a man to progress beyond his current state, make him see beyond his current state. If you want a man to think differently, make him see differently. If you will maximise the potentials of your seeds, you need a clear vision that is void of ambiguities. You need to see the world beyond your nest and not only from the perspective of your nest. You need

LAUNCH OUT WITH A PURPOSE

to have a perspective of the world beyond your family, discipline, calling, church denomination and nation. A man with a great vision and focus is a limitless man. You underestimate such a man at your own detriment.

> **And the Lord said unto Abram, after that Lot was separated from him, lift up now thine eyes, and look from the place where thou art northward, and southward, and eastward, and westward: For all the land which thou seest, to thee will I give it, and to thy seed for ever**
> **– Genesis 13: 14 - 15 (KJV)**

According to Genesis 13: 15, whatever land God was to give to Abraham was dependent on Abraham's ability to sight it. His harvests and that of his dependants were predicated on the clarity and the depth of his vision. How much land do you think Abraham was able to see with his naked eyes? Our eyes may be limited but our vision is limitless. Until you can interpret your vision, you may not be able to actualise it. Your harvest is largely a product of your vision. Your sight is a function of your physical eyes, but your vision is the function of your spirit man.

The Holy Bible says, **"where there is no vision, the people perish"** Proverbs 29: 18a (KJV). That means at every point in your life you need a fresh vision and a new perspective to thrive. When there is no vision or where your vision is blurred, disaster is lurking at the corner.

#The only thing worse than being blind is
having sight but no vision.
—Helen Keller

There are many people with good eyesight who have no vision; they are walking aimlessly through life. The danger of having no vision for your seed, which is your life is that you deprive yourself and generations yet unborn the privilege of partaking in the harvest. You should understand there are a lot of lives attached to yours. Launch out with a purpose to sow your seeds today!

CHAPTER 3

PROTECT YOUR SEED

As he was scattering the seed, some fell along the path, and the birds came and ate it up. Mark 4: 4 (NIV)

AS THE FARMER SOWED, some seeds fell along the way side. Because they were exposed and unprotected the fowls of the air devoured them. There is a need to be conscious and aware of the gifts and the seeds God has deposited in you. God expects maximum use of your seeds no matter how much or little you think they are. The farmer was not conscious of getting maximum harvests from all his seeds. No seed is a waste, and this is exactly how you should approach different areas of your life. Everything that matters in life begins with a seed and must be grown: business, family, marriage, relationship, etc.

There are many aspects of life you may have given up because you are yet to see any visible fruit whereas they are still at their budding stages. Sometimes we work on areas of our lives that always yield results easily and abandon other areas because we feel it is a waste of time to dedicate resources to them, especially if we had failed in the past in such areas. The truth is that they are all seeds and seeds vary. Some seeds need extra care and nurturing to yield good harvests, some need less monitoring. Some take a longer period of time to yield harvests while some take shorter period. Some need very little resources to thrive; others require more resources to thrive. Some seeds can germinate when exposed to water; others can only germinate when buried in the soil. The point here is simple, different seeds need different approach to get the required harvests.

For instance, many parents give up the role of parenting after so much effort because they feel they are failing. They would rather channel their resources towards other areas of lives like business, career, et al to the detriment of the family. Since their efforts at parenting do not seem to yield any positive results, they conclude that successful parenting is beyond their reach and so they give up. They may approach parenting like other areas of their lives forgetting that these are different seeds and certainly require different approach. You should realise the lives of your children, spouse and loved ones God has given to you are seeds and how you nurture them today will reflect on your harvests tomorrow. You can always continue from where you stopped and from where you failed, it's never too late.

#It is never too late to plant and nurture your seed.

One danger of not protecting your seed is that the birds of the air could eat them up. Devourers are ever busy looking for seeds to devour (1st Peter 5: 8). As a child, I observed how my mother preserved maize seeds to plant at the home garden. She kept them dry and away from our reach. One fateful day, my baby sister got hold of the seeds and took them outside the house to the backyard and was playing with them. She exposed the seeds and it wasn't long when stray hens found the maize seeds and descended on them. After that incident, my mother became more deliberate and conscious in preserving her seeds. Whenever she got maize seeds, she would put them safely in a container with a lid and instructed us to steer clear of the container. It was clear to all that she was deliberately preserving the seeds for a purpose. Protect and care for your seeds consciously and deliberately as if your survival depends on them. Of course, your seed is your life. Let everyone around you know that you mean business with your seeds and you are not ready to play games with them. Let people around you know what is important to you; let them know what you value; what your principles and convictions are and where you stand. God doesn't expect you to be careless and reckless with whatever He has given you.

Sin is not a Joke

Living a life of sin is being careless with your seeds. Samson is an example of one who was careless with his seed. He did not protect it rather he exposed it to his enemies and ended up dying with them. The number of people who died with him were more than those he killed in his lifetime. In other words, at the time of his death, his seeds were still untapped and fresh. There was still a lot of harvests to reap from his seeds but recklessness and carelessness made him to lose out of his harvests. Carelessness with your seeds could cost your life; it could cause irreversible damage to your existence. Anytime you are faced with making a decision about breaking the laws of God, ask yourself "will this decision or action, take me farther away from God or closer? Will it expose my seeds to danger?" When you play with sin, you dine with the devil and when you dine with the devil, you will be spiritually mal-nourished. Sin dampens your soul and separates your spirit from God. If you want to go through life expressing and making good use of the seeds God has deposited in you, you need to always be in tune with Him. Sin disconnects you from God who is your ultimate source. The world today has commercialised sin thus making it trendy, fash-ionable and desirable. This doesn't change the fact that sin is sin. It doesn't matter who says it is not, it doesn't matter how it has been packaged or refined, it doesn't matter how much revelation of God's grace you now have, sin remains sin. When you allow sin to creep into your life, it drains and robs you of your seeds in bits. You would think you are in control of life until you are totally drawn away and you lose all your seeds.

The Little Foxes

> **Take us the foxes, THE LITTLE FOXES,**
> **THAT SPOIL THE VINES: for our vines**
> **have tender grapes. (BOLD mine)**
> **-Song of Solomon 2: 15 (KJV)**

Often times I have realised it is the 'little' sins here and there left unchecked that accumulate and become the bigger problem for believers. They constitute the little foxes that eventually spoil the vine. They are the little foxes that destroy the vineyard and kill the fruits with their seeds. How terrible! Little foxes are those sins that easily beset a person, that which easily exposes a person and make them vulnerable to satanic attacks. The 'smallest' of sins can make one lose one's seed, derail destiny and keep one in perpetual bondage. Sin has the power to take you out of God's master plan for your life and destiny. It has the tendency to rob you of your intimacy with God. The birds of the air came for the seeds that fell on the path but not the seeds that were planted or the ones in the hands of the farmer. The devourer comes for your seed in moments of your vulnerability; in moments of fear and despair, in moments when you let your guard down, in moments when you compromise on your beliefs. At such moments, you are exposed without any covering and without any defence. I recall a Christian movie we watched as children titled **Just a Little Sin**. The storyline was about a music minister who by all account was destined for greatness but lost her precious seeds because of one night of fornication. She lost her calling and lost her life in the process without fulfilling her destiny. The seemingly little sins have grave consequences as any other 'bigger' one you can ever think of because the consequences remain the same namely death (Romans 6: 23). Therefore, there is no small or big sin. If you put a drop of cyanide or any other harmful chemical into pure water, will that water remain pure? The answer is obvious. You cannot continuously and knowingly engage in 'drops of sin' and not expect to put your precious seeds at risk. Our God is all forgiving and He proved His love for us in that while we were yet sinners, Christ died for us (Romans 5: 8). There is no doubt about the fact that you could obtain forgiveness if you truly repent but you may never recover your lost seed. Why take such risk then?

> **So, if you think you are standing firm, be careful that you don't fall. -1st Corinthians 10: 12 (NIV)**

We are prone to falling and making mistakes when we rely on our own strength to stand. We must therefore realise that the strength we need to stand comes from God. To protect your seeds, you have to be totally dependent on God. You should neither depend on your own understanding nor put your trust in the flesh and your abilities so that when the prince of this world shows up, you would not be vulnerable (John 14: 30).

Never give him any legal ground to tamper with your seed.

#Protection and care for your seed is your responsibility

Other little foxes we need to protect our seeds from include: a little sleep, a little faith and despising of small beginnings.

A Little Sleep

> **Yet a little sleep, a little slumber, a little folding of the hands to sleep: 34 So shall thy poverty come as one that travelleth; and thy want as an armed man. Proverbs 24: 33 - 34 (KJV)**

Sleep is good and God enables man to rest effectively by sleeping. Sleep helps the body to function optimally, recuperate, reduce stress and improve mood. It also helps to reduce the risk of having serious health problems. "Many things that we take for granted are affected by sleep. If you sleep better, you can certainly live better. It's pretty clear." says Raymonde Jean. There is no doubt about the effectiveness of a sound sleep towards our well-being. However, we must never forget to look at the negative consequences of oversleeping.

"Similar to people who sleep too little, people who sleep too much have higher overall mortality risks" – Dr Michael Breus. Apart from the risk to our health when we oversleep, we risk killing our seeds. When you spend the most part of your precious time sleeping, chances are that you will never achieve or reach any major goal or dream in life. If you allow a little sleep to steal your time, there will never be enough time left for you to work on your seeds, cultivate and enjoy bountiful harvests. **"If the average night's sleep is eight hours (i.e. one third of a day), one sleeps for one third of one's life. If you live, say, 75 years, that's 25 years of sleep, or 9,125 days"** according to Max Wurr. Interesting, isn't it? You basically have 50 years left for other areas of life. If you go further to subtract the time spent in other activities out of the 50, it is easy to see we really do not have as much time as we think we do. That's how people begin from a little sleep until it becomes a deadly habit which would eventually lead to a bigger problem known as poverty! Many will wake up at old age to wonder how or why their life turned out so badly. If the truth must be told, it is probably that they spent their productive years sleeping or engaging in activities that did not contribute towards the growth of their seeds. If you are an excessive sleeper, you may find it difficult to meet your daily needs. In that case, fulling purpose and achieving destiny would become a herculean task.

I recall as a teenager, I was inspired by the story of a very successful man in his fifties; he was an old student of my high school. Along with two friends of his who were equally alumnus of our school, they decided to visit us to reminisce their days as students. As they took a walk around the school blocks, they met my friends and I exchanging banter in one of the classrooms. After we exchanged pleasantries with them, he gave us a mini pep talk on why we should take our studies seriously. He told us that he made up his mind as a teenager never to be a slave all his life who would only be working to pay bills and never living a life of fulfilment. He said this decision helped him to be strategic, take his studies seriously, work hard as a young man and retire early enough to pursue his dreams. He added that one of the decisions he took to achieve his goal was cutting down on excessive sleeping habit. He had been so diligent that at his age, he did not need to work to pay his bills anymore in life. People who are in the habit of sleeping excessively are setting themselves up to be slaves when they should be leaders. It would be devastating and sad when you should be leading, but you end up labouring because you spent your productive years in excessive sleep. Proverbs 12: 24 puts it in very clear terms: **"Work hard and become a leader; be lazy and become a slave"** (NLT). A little sleep is one of the little foxes we must guard against otherwise our precious seeds of time which God has given to us could be stolen and never to be recovered.

A Little Faith

> **Immediately Jesus reached out his hand and caught him. "You of little faith," he said, "why did you doubt?" Matthew 14: 31 (NIV)**

Another little fox, we constantly need to guard against is 'little faith'. Having little faith is different from unbelief. Unbelief is being in a constant state of doubt and not acknowledging or trusting God. However, having 'little faith' is doubting God in some specific situations or circumstances. Little faith is as ineffective as having no faith at all. Little faith could be more dangerous in that it is enough to make you take the first right step forward but unable to get you to your desired destination. It's like putting your hand on the plough and then looking back. (Luke 9: 62). How dangerous! Peter had faith to step into the water. He took a few steps forward but hadn't enough faith to stay afloat. No wonder Jesus described his faith as little. He saw the waves and the wind, fear kicked in and he began to drown. Thankfully, Jesus had mercy on him and stretched out His hand to help him. Your seed will drown and be buried in the challenges of this world if you do not exercise enough faith in God when you step out to sow and grow your seed. Peter's little faith would have been disastrous if it wasn't Jesus that beckoned on him to walk on the sea. We have no reason to doubt our God when we take that first step towards growing our seed because; it is our God that deposited those seeds in us and instructed us to be fruitful and multiply. Doubt would spoil things for us if we are not acting according to God's command and instructions but trusting in our own flesh, strength and understanding. It is the will of God that you grow your seeds and the will of God will not lead you to where His grace will not be sufficient for you. Whenever you find yourself in doubt, the first question you should ask yourself is: "what is God's mind or instruction about this situation?" To find out God's mind, consult the Holy Bible. There will always be turbulent waves and destructive winds that will appear or attempt to put your seed in great danger. However, the greater risk for your seed is having little faith in the One who gave you those seeds.

#The will of God will not lead you to where His grace will not be sufficient for you

The comforting lesson from the story in Matthew 14 is that Peter cried out to Jesus when he started drowning and Jesus heard his cry. Whenever you find your faith waning, get on your knees and cry out to God, He will answer you (Psalm 50:15). I have had times in my life that I cried to God to increase my faith and He did. At some point, even the apostles said to Jesus "increase our faith!" (Luke 17: 5). Asking God to increase your faith might be a very significant prayer that you may need to pray as you seek to cultivate your seed. We are sometimes likely to pray for storms to cease. It can be understandable because storms are unpleasant, destructive and pose a great risk to our seeds. But when your faith is increased, you will ride the storm and waves to your advantage and nothing will stop you from making progress with your seeds. You need to cry out to God to help you walk on the water amidst the waves because you just have to keep walking otherwise you risk getting drowned. To protect your seed, you must guard against little faith because little faith could get you up and running but it is not likely to be sufficient to keep you afloat.

Despising little beginnings

> Do not despise these small be-
> ginnings, for the Lord rejoices
> to see the work begin, to see the
> plumb line in Zerubbabel's hand.
> - Zechariah 4:10 (NLT)

It is difficult to conceive how anyone intends to grow his seed by despising little beginnings because seeds by their very nature are 'little'. 'Little beginnings' serve their own purpose in our seed growing undertaking. Despising little beginnings therefore is simply being naïve and outrightly foolish. Despising little beginnings means you are short sighted and can't see into the future. Nature teaches us 'little beginnings' in almost every aspect of life. For instance, human life begins as a tiny cell and so does a big orange tree with hundreds of fruits. Little beginnings are integral part of our existence. We should therefore embrace, nurture and cherish those moments because they never last forever rather they are the foundation for great harvests. People who tend to mock and despise little beginnings never get to achieve anything significant in life because they tend to be afraid of being stuck at the level they mocked, scorned and criticised others. As you embark on your seed sowing exercise, avoid people who are fond of despising little beginnings; people who always try to poke holes into your dreams, visions and goals. They can make you see only problems without proffering any solution and you could lose sight of your destination. Rather than despise little beginnings, thank God for them, having it at the back of your mind that it is God that gives the growth. Jesus lifted up His eyes and thanked the Father for the five loaves and two fishes. He knew that for the provision, His Father was worthy of thanks. Following the thanksgiving, the food was enough to feed more than five thousand people with twelve baskets of leftover (Luke 9: 16, 17). Others saw five loaves and two fishes only, but Jesus saw beyond the five loaves and two fishes; He saw the increase that would arise from them. What you think is too small or too little for God to work with is what God can multiply if only you won't despise it but give thanks and get down to work. Everyone sees and admires fruit trees standing tall in all their glory with fruits on them but no one sees the days and times when these trees were just seeds waiting to be cultivated. No one sees the effort of the farmer that did the cultivation. Whenever I have the rare opportunity to meet great minds or people who have made giant strides in their domain, I am always curious to know what they did during the times when they were unknown and insignificant. Call it their days of little beginnings. Many times, the latter glory we see is the product of diligence, persistence, hard work, mistakes and errors in the days of little beginnings. **"For the Lord rejoices to see the work begin..."** this means we should also rejoice in the times of small beginnings. We rejoice because we know we have a direction and a destination as we begin the journey. Protect your seed and learn to rejoice in your little beginnings.

Guard your heart

> **Above all else, guard your heart,**
> **for everything you do flows from**
> **it - Proverbs 4:23 (NIV)**

One effective way to protect and care for your seed is to guard your heart. The heart is the engine room of our thoughts and actions; it is the stronghold of a man's life. From the heart proceeds wisdom, emotions, attitude and conduct. The human heart is an important organ of the body. When and if it is unhealthy, the whole body would be in jeopardy. In the same vein, when you do not guard your heart you can destroy your precious seeds. Personally, I test the words of people by their actions. People could say anything they want you to hear but you can only know the true state of their hearts by their actions. Jesus

understood this when he said '**These people honour me with their lips, but their hearts are far
from me**" (Matthew 15: 8). What you do reveals
more about what you think than what you say. To
effectively guard your heart, you must be sensitive to what you allow to settle on your mind and
who you give access to your heart. One way the
scripture shows us how to guard our heart is by
renewing our minds with the word of God.

> **Do not conform to the pattern
> of this world but be transformed
> by the renewing of your mind.
> Then you will be able to test and
> approve what God's will is—his
> good, pleasing and perfect will
> - Romans 12:2 (NIV)**

If we do not make any conscious effort to see
that our hearts aren't polluted and manipulated,
we would find ourselves carrying out actions
that would expose our seeds to danger. Samson
couldn't guard his heart rather he exposed it to
Delilah. If there was one-person Samson shouldn't
have exposed his heart to, it was Delilah. She was
after his precious seeds whereas he was clueless.
He became vulnerable to her when he let down his
guards. He told her all his heart: "**there hath not
come a razor upon mine head; for I have been a**

Nazarite unto God from my mother's womb..." Judges 16: 17 (KJV). Many people have given and exposed their hearts to the wrong people and some are yet to recover from the betrayal that followed. When the bird steals your exposed seeds, it is a daunting task to recover them. Who are you discussing your God given ideas with? Who are your confidants? Who do you share your dreams with? Who do you discuss your revelations with? Who do you reveal your strength to? Who do you reveal your weaknesses to? Who are you sharing your family secrets with? Who do you share the innermost part of your heart with? Matters of the heart shouldn't be taken lightly. It is for this reason important decisions such as choosing a life partner shouldn't be taken in haste or blindly. You'll literally be sharing your heart and exposing your seeds to whoever you become one with. If they are with you for the wrong reasons, sooner or later, they will break your heart and take a piece of it with them. Be it marriage, business relationships, mentor-mentee relationships, etc. one must exercise utmost care. All relationships should be approached with adequate preparation, information and awareness. Remember you want to ultimately protect your seeds from being stolen or exploited. Some people have experienced heart breaks which they never fully recovered from; it ruined them and took them to their early graves. For others, it followed them all through life into old age. They basically lived the latter part of their lives in misery and regrets. God wants your heart (Proverbs 23: 26) and it is no surprise that the devil also is after the heart because he knows that it is from there great ideas and wisdom spring forth. He knows the ultimate security of your seeds is when your heart is one with God in a faithful and committed relationship. The devil knows if he can snatch your heart from God, he can steal your precious seeds. So what do you do? Protect your precious seeds by guarding your heart!

CHAPTER 4

CULTIVATE YOUR SOIL

Some fell on rocky places, where it did not have much soil. It sprang up quickly, because the soil was shallow. Mark 4: 5 (NIV)

CULTIVATING YOUR SOIL MEANS to till, dig, stir, overturn, break up, prepare and give special attention, care and time to your soil with a view to having bountiful harvests. Your soil is the environment or resource your seeds need to thrive in. Any good farmer knows the soil is an important resource needed for the seeds to germinate and bear fruits. The seeds God has given you need valuable resources to germinate and yield fruits but sometimes we are in a haste to plant without first examining the resource and what it will take to sow the seeds successfully. The soil carries nutrients that the seeds require for germination. The role of the soil in planting cannot be overemphasised. You cannot plant your seeds while neglecting what is required for the seeds to grow. The soil must be enriched while doing away with toxic materials at the same time. For instance, if you have a land you want to cultivate, you could dig some soil from the land and send it to agricultural agencies for testing. After testing, they would send you a report on the nutritional composition of your soil. With the aid of all kinds of modern agricultural technologies, farmers are able to test the nutritional contents of the soil to grow their crops. What's the purpose of this test? It gives you an insight into what you can cultivate on that soil. It determines what nutrients are lacking, in what quantity and how you can compensate for or introduce what's lacking into the soil for a better yield. Similarly, learn to test or examine all the resources at your disposal in your seed sowing agenda. You cannot afford to be careless and waste your effort without a deserving harvest. Examine what you have to be sure of what you'll need to cultivate your soil.

Godly Self Introspection

Cultivating your soil can also mean learning to self-introspect, to ask yourself questions that help you cross examine yourself in the light of God's word. Use the word of God to probe yourself; your true intentions, how you see yourself, your weak points, your struggles, your strength, your interest, your talents, your gifts, your passion, your past mistakes, your failures, your successes, your dreams, and your calling. What is the purpose of all these? To give you an insight into what you have, what you need to improve upon, where you are going and what you need or can do to get there. In summary, self-introspection reveals your weaknesses and strengths. Knowing your weakness gives you a glimpse into what you should do and knowing your strength encourages you. Ask yourself questions such as;

- What has God called me to do?
- What drives or motivates me?
- What sin easily besets me?
- What am I passionate about?
- What do I fear most?
- What gifts and talents do I have?
- What are my hopes and desires?
- What are my dreams and aspirations?
- Are my hopes, desires, dreams and aspirations self-centred and can they stand the scrutiny of God's word?
- How can I effectively use my gifts and talents to serve God and humanity?

- What are the promises of God for my life?
- Is my heart with God?
- What support system do I have?
- What does the scripture say about me?
- What do people say I am good at?
- What do I think I am good at?
- What am I very poor at?
- What do people tend to criticise me for?
- What areas of my life can I improve upon?
- What have I learned from my past failures and mistakes?
- What did I do the last time I succeeded and how can I replicate or apply it elsewhere?
- How have I been beneficial to my friends?
- How have I served my community?
- How do I want to serve my community?
- Why do I want to do this business or undertake this vocation or career?
- What do I do happily without expecting any form of reward, payment or compensation?
- What do I feel fulfilled doing?
- What do people tend to approach me for/ about?
- What traits from my parents do I find in myself?
- What character do my parents exhibit that I now find in me?

- What made my parents' marriage success-ful or not so successful?
- What is my family known for?
- What is my family good at?
- Who influences me easily and why?
- Who do I influence and why?
- Why are people drawn towards me or away from me?
- And what does the scripture say about my concerns and the answers I seek?

The questions are endless. You need to ask yourself relevant questions and allow the Word of God to guide you towards the answers you seek. When you self-introspect, don't forget you are not doing it to be self-centred but to prepare yourself to maximize the seeds God has depos-ited in you to reach your potentials, fulfil purpose and glorify Him. Be careful that you do not get yourself into self-pity and depression while intro-specting. It should be a healthy self-examination and not a pity party or an avenue to look down on yourself or feel inferior to others. The goal is not to make you feel bad about yourself but to understand yourself and the opportunities and resources God has made available to you. It is best to self-introspect from the lenses of God's Word where you can receive answers. Through this, you can glean a better perspective or be led on

how to get the answers you need. Use the word of
God to dig deep into your life so you do not set
out to sow your seeds without any knowledge of
who you are, what you have, where you are now
and where you are going. It requires humility and
honesty for you to let the word of God be the
benchmark for your self-introspection. You can't
shrink, downplay or ignore whatever is revealed
to you that needs change; acknowledge this is truly who you are and pray the prayer of the Palmist:

> **Search me, God, and know my
> heart; test me and know my
> anxious thoughts.**[24] **See if there
> is any offensive way in me, and
> lead me in the way everlasting.
> Psalm 139: 23 - 24 (NIV)**

After self-introspection, learn to take action
and build from there. As you pray from a sincere
heart for God to lead you, He will direct your
path. This will only happen when you are sincere
and truly willing to take concrete steps to make
the required sacrifices. Not everyone is willing to
make the required sacrifices. Some literally break
up their soil and leave it that way without taking the necessary steps to prepare the soil for the
planting of their seeds.

Anyone who listens to the word but does not do what it says is like someone who looks at his face in a mirror[24] and, after looking at himself, goes away and immediately forgets what he looks like.[25] But whoever looks intently into the perfect law that gives freedom and continues in it—not forgetting what they have heard, but doing it—they will be blessed in what they do. James 1: 23 -25 (NIV)

The knowledge of the Word of God does not transform you until you act on it. Your reward will only come from taking the necessary action after you have looked inward and discovered your shallow areas. By not taking any action, you may forget what you are and you may be heading for a terrible poor harvest. When you do not take action, it means you have failed to cultivate your soil, it means you are on a journey of empty dreams. I like what Proverbs 28:19 (NIV) says about this: **"Those who work their land will have abundant food, but those who chase fantasies will have their fill of poverty"**. Notice it does not say: "those who work their seed" but it says "those who work their land (soil)". Just as cultivating or tilling the soil is an important step in seeds planting, self-introspection in the light of God's word is also an important step in our seeds sowing effort. The major reason farmers cultivate the soil is to put it in the best physical condition for the seeds to germinate and thrive. Self-introspection in the light of God's word puts you in the right state of mind and condition for your seeds to germinate and thrive.

As said earlier, the Holy Bible remains the best book for self-discovery. I had a personal experience in my late teenage years after a continuous and deliberate effort at understanding the totality of the life God has given me. Teenage is usually a time of curiosity, exploration and self-assertion. The Word of God helped me to navigate successfully through that period of my life leading me into making choices that would not mar my destiny. I began to understand my duties to myself, my family, and my community and the indispensability of God in fulfilling these responsibilities. The truth about God's word is that it will never lie to you. People could tell you what they think you want to hear or what they believe will be pleasing to you, they may lie to you about you but the word of God will reveal who and what you are to you without any filter. Your family and community may attempt to define you by the failings, shortcomings and mistakes of your parents and generations before you but God's word will open your mind to the truth about God's purpose for your life which is not predicated on any circumstance of your life. The truth about your life begins with God's unconditional love for you irrespective of your sins, race, tribe, ethnicity and location on the planet.

Count the cost

In 2014, I was planning a trip to Lithuania in Eastern Europe where I was to continue my bachelor's degree programme. People who know me well know that I am very meticulous when it comes to planning trips. I try to predict every possible scenario and prepare for them. I was offered various flight fares and options for the trip by my travel agents. Some had longer layovers within my budget while some had shorter layovers which were a bit more expensive but still fairly within the average flight cost for the route. As my travel agents listed the fare for each ticket they could find, I wasn't patient enough to listen to all the options available. I requested for the cheapest flight ticket available. I was young so I felt I could withstand a long tiring journey so I refused to bother about other important details that could impact on me negatively during the trip such as the layover time, layover airport and the airline. The fare was my major concern but what I did not understand is the fact that comfort must be considered in every journey and that I could pay dearly for any discomfort. I ended up flying a route with an eight-hour layover twice. It was a tiring and exhausting sixteen-hour layover of which in one of the airports, the facilities provided for layovers were not conducive. I won't bore you with the details of the treatment I received from the border police at one of the airports, the abysmal service by the airline and their old passenger plane. I was full of regrets for choosing the cheapest ticket in the market as I arrived at my destination disoriented and cranky. I later discovered there was enough information out there from the unpleasant experiences of previous passengers about the airline and one of the layover airports. If I had done my due diligence and not made a choice solely based on the cheap airfare, I could have made a better choice. I thought I was being prudent by purchasing the cheapest ticket but little did I know that it would turn out to be an expensive choice. For me the cost of the trip meant only the fare. This particular incident taught me important lessons one of which is that I must not travel without having adequate information about transit/transfer airports when travelling with a third world passport. I share this story to demonstrate that counting the cost is beyond monetary or quantum value.

For which of you, intending to build a tower, sitteth not down first, and counteth the cost, whether he have sufficient to finish it? Luke 14:28 (KJV)

Taking good time to research and count the cost before embarking on any project is highly beneficial both at the long and short run. It will prepare you for possible challenges and save you serious embarrassment. It is worrisome that we always tend to count the cost before we go shopping for groceries, or before we approach a car dealership or before we do things that have temporal impact on our lives but we rarely put in the deserved effort to count the cost before we make life altering and sometimes irreversible life decisions. Perhaps if we were to look at our lives as living seed, we would probably be more guided. It is always costly to count the cost. And to count the cost is a deliberate effort. When counting the cost, consider the possible gains, the liabilities, and the sacrifices you have to make. Enumerate the resources at your disposal and contingency plans in an event of failure or unforeseen circumstances. Consider those who might be directly or indirectly impacted by the action or decision you are about to take; weigh the possible impact or outcome on their lives. In other words, look at the bigger picture. Your seed can only yield harvest as much as your soil can carry; that is why it is wise to prepare and cultivate your soil adequately. Preparation before you begin planting your seed is a must; you cannot substitute it for anything or it may cost you everything at the end. Counting the cost could also mean seeking knowledge, information about what it will take to get your desired harvests. There is a cost for everything; there is a price to be paid because nothing great comes cheap most of the time. If you don't sit down, count the cost and improve the planting environment, your knowledge and understanding in planting, you would have indirectly set yourself up for failure. The seed in Mark 4: 5 sprang up quickly and died because the soil was shallow. Here lies the danger of sowing in a shallow soil. How many times have you begun implementing an idea, a dream or a plan without the knowledge or required depth to sustain it? For your seed to survive, you need to understand the environment it needs. Many businesses have failed not because they were destined to fail but because people launch into business without the required depth they need to succeed. Some launch into business without understanding the business and industry they want to be part of. For instance, you need a certain level of depth and knowledge in understanding the kind of business you want to execute, how the market works, who the big players and thought leaders in the industry are, who the market shareholders are, what the consumers want, who your competitors are or will be, what value is missing in the current market, what your product or service differentiation is and what value you want to offer your customers. When you have the depth of information and knowledge you need, it will help you sow your seed appropriately and when you cultivate your soil, you are simply preparing a good harvest from your seed.

Many marriages fail because people hopped into it without the resources, depth and knowledge of what the union entails. Many people are shallow minded and because they fail to develop themselves, progress becomes elusive. For instance, they begin to celebrate and party at the slightest victory when the battle is far from being over let alone being won. They are motivated by superficial things like latest flashy cars just to appear successful in the eye of the public. You don't embark on a project or a cause because of the superficial value or ostentatious lifestyle you expect to get when you don't have the resources to pursue it to a logical conclusion. Learn to count the cost.

Be patient; increase your capacity

The shallow soil in Mark 4: 5 did not have enough capacity to sustain the seed after germination. Learn to increase your capacity in your relationship with God, your subordinates, superiors, friends, acquaintances, associates and partners. Growing your knowledge of people, finance, environment, yourself, calling, career or profession are very crucial. What you can sustain largely depends on your capacity for sustainability. The seeds 'sprang up quickly' but did not survive. We are in a generation where everyone wants to rise fast. Everyone wants a quick rise but no patience to cultivate the soil and provide an enabling environment that is not 'rocky' to grow the seeds. For instance, 14 months after planting a well grafted mango seedling, it would yield flowers but the farmer would pluck them off. If the flowers are left, the plant would yield some mango fruits no doubt. The next season, the plant would yield flowers and the farmer would pluck them off again. The mango farmer waits deliberately for the plant to grow into a full-fledged tree before allowing it to bear fruits because he knows that if it bears fruit at that early stage, it would not grow into a tree that can bear enough fruits. In other words, the plant would not grow and bear fruits to its maximal potential or capacity. This wise farming technique teaches that rushing to rise without adequate preparation and patience will stunt growth and reduce harvests in the long run. The technological revolution we are experiencing in all spheres of human endeavour isn't helping matters in terms of how impatient we have become. Every aspect of life is now being affected by what I call 'on-demand' culture because we are increasingly dependent on and conditioned by technology. We are beginning to cultivate 'on-demand' habits.

There was a time you had to prepare, plan, buy a ticket and book a seat to go watch blockbuster movies at the cinema but in today's world, you can watch the latest release of great movies from the comfort of your living room on-demand. With a click on your device from the comfort of your home, you can buy a brand-new car and have it delivered to your doorsteps. While there is no doubt these technological innovations have greatly improved our livelihood, however, we are gradually becoming more impatient with life in general. Youths who haven't really invested in their lives are getting dissatisfied and impatient with life because they are constantly seeing the flamboyant lifestyle of others and wishing it could be them. No thanks to the social media. There are young people who are at their first jobs but crave the lifestyle of someone who has been working for decades. Some of the things people greatly admire, or desire would eventually come if only they would patiently cultivate their own soil, sow their own seed and be patient to allow the plant to grow into a fully developed tree ready to bear fruits. We are in that time when many do not have the patience to wait for their seed to die in the soil for proper germination. Most want to achieve so much in life within a very short period of time and preferably at a very young age. There is absolutely nothing wrong in making giant strides early in life, business, career or profession but it is good to be sure one has all it takes; the resources and the tenacity to remain relevant for as long as possible while improving and building on what one has already achieved. Hard work is needed to be successful and harder work is required to remain successful. It is no surprise very successful people always stay successful, because they have developed a habit of dedicating more resources and building capacity.

In the parable of the talents in Matthew 25: 14 - 30, do you ever wonder why the servant who was successful and made five more talents was given the talent of the servant who refused to invest the only talent he had? The servant who had ten talents had clearly shown he had the capacity to bring about increase and sustainability. You may never know what capacity you would build, what you would discover about yourself, the new

experiences and skills you may gain as you cultivate your soil.

At a time in my life as a teenager; I invested
my little pocket money in acquiring information
by going to the internet café to search for universities around the world that had degree programmes within my area of interest. Within a
very short time, I had a good knowledge of what
it would cost me financially and how to apply
for degree programmes in different parts of the
world. One fateful day, I was surprised to meet
someone who got paid to help prospective students apply for degree programmes in various
universities abroad. It looked absurd to me, this
information was all over the internet, a simple
google search would lead you to the website of
any university in the world and you would access any relevant information you need to make
a successful application. Why would anyone be
willing to pay for information he can readily access for free? (Though internet data is not free)
But this fellow made me understand some people
are just lazy or not tech savvy or do not have the
luxury of time but would rather pay someone to
get them the information they need and guide
them through the process of applying for admis-
sion and placement into universities abroad. I had
no idea I could earn a passive income from the
information I had gathered over time. When I set

out to research before applying for degree pro-grammes, was I planning to earn money from the information I was going to gather? Definitely not. My point is simple, the gains you could make and the lessons you could learn while cultivating your soil are added advantage in the long run.

#It's easy to rise but difficult to stand.
You need double the effort you employ to
get to the top to stay at the top.

Verily, verily, I say unto you, ex-cept a corn of wheat fall into the ground and die, it abideth alone: but if it die, it bringeth forth much fruit- John 12: 24 (KJV)

The process and time it takes for a seed to die, could be long. It is during this process the seed establishes its root and depth which is why the soil is very important. A rocky soil could pose problems especially if the seeds are not adapted to such environment. Imbibe the habit of patient-ly developing yourself to the point where nothing can make you fizzle out but to meet your goals and hit your targets. If for instance, you make up your mind to be a medical doctor, you probably have the potentials to be one but until you pass through medical school successfully, you would never become one. The process of becoming a medical doctor is challenging, your life would revolve around the lecture rooms, library, laboratory and teaching hospital for years until those places and what you learn there become part of you. You would need to transit from the point of studying to pass exams to the point of studying to gain practical knowledge that can be applied to save lives. You learn, unlearn, retain, improve and so on and so forth. You literally die to your desire and pleasures. You may not be able to do what everyone does because your gaze is set on the future harvests you are 'dying' to germinate and grow. This is delayed gratification and it entails discipline, patience, hard work, diligence and consistency. The concept of delayed gratification is foreign to many in this age and we can see the results all around us. We are raising a generation that pursues instant gratification at the expense of important pursuits of a life time. Delayed gratification must be taught to children if they would grow to become responsible adults in the future.

When I was in high school, I couldn't phantom how or why some of my peers who had bad grades sacrificed the time for their home work to play football. As a child, I was taught by my parents to put away something pleasurable now in order to gain something much more rewarding later. In fact, one of my motivations towards doing what I needed to do was the joy and peace I knew would be mine if I prioritise. I recall whenever it was examination period in school my mother would not let us watch any of our regular TV programmes or sitcom until our examinations were over. In our minds, we knew after successfully completing our examinations, we would be allowed to watch our favourite TV programmes. This was a simple but effective method to teach us delayed gratification. The ability to delay gratification is lacking in many adults because they were never taught or trained on how to deny their flesh for the moment what they want. If you must effectively work with the seeds God has deposited in you, you have to put your flesh under subjection (1st Corinthians 9: 27). When we live in pursuit of immediate pleasure, we are not different from babies. The flesh always desires pleasure and constantly fights anything that would be gainful. Oh yes, putting your flesh under subjection to do your will comes with pain but such are the pains that would be rewarding at the long run. One interesting fact about learning to delay gratification is that it would benefit you in multiple dimensions: health wise, finance, career, marriage, and etc. When practised consistently, it becomes part of one's character. Delayed gratification teaches priority setting and enhances positive outcome. You cannot afford to be disorderly with your priorities and expect plausible harvests from your seeds. Every meaningful and rewarding pursuit is achieved by a deliberate and orderly execution. Cultivating your soils means you are identifying and taking the required steps towards sowing your seeds.

> **Those who work their land will have abundant food, but those who chase fantasies have no sense – Proverbs 12: 11(NIV)**

God has blessed man with abundant arable land to grow food but he has to till it to make it suitable for planting. In the same vein, God has blessed us with all the tools, knowledge and resources we need to cultivate our 'soil' so that our seeds could flourish. Never forget that if you leave your soil unattended to, you would have no harvest when you need it most. Cultivate your soil by godly self-introspection. Count the cost of sowing your seeds and be patient to increase your capacity in order to maximize your seeds.

CHAPTER 5

YOUR SEED NEEDS
ROOT

But when the sun came up, the plants were scorched, and they withered because they had no root. Mark 4:5-6 (NIV)

THE PLANTS DID NOT wither because of the heat of the Sun they withered because they had no roots. The roots of a plant are under the ground, unseen but very crucial to the survival of the plant. They grow constantly reaching deep into the soil and spreading wide. The roots keep the plant stable, to absorb, store and transports nutrients and water from the soil to the whole plant to

117

keep it healthy for continuous growth. The root is the first part of the plant that is formed; it can reproduce a new shoot even when a plant is cut down. In essence, the root is the foundation of a plant.

As we sow our seeds, we must remember that God is our foundation. He comes first because He is our root. High school biology teaches that plants need water, air, nutrients and sunlight to grow. But in Mark 4: 6 we realise that sunlight could pose problems for a plant if it has no roots. So, irrespective of the availability of water, air, nutrients and sunlight, if the plants have no foundation (root), its survival is threatened. When your seed goes through the process of germination and it is solidly rooted in God, what is a disadvantage to others would become an advantage to you. The same sunlight that is needed for the growth of plants is the same sunlight that withers other plants without roots. Having depth is the secret to turning a disadvantage to an advantage. For instance, an individual with a good in-depth knowledge of practical finance or business knows where to make investments when an economy is plummeting and while others are complaining. This also shows that it is not wise to compare your challenge and situation with that of other people. On the surface, the plant with depth (root) and the plant without depth may look alike but it takes only the continuous heat and light of the sun over time to separate them because intrinsically one was bound to outlive the other because it had root. Sometimes when two individuals go through the same situation, one might come out becoming better, while the other comes out worse for it. I grew up hearing my father use this saying in some of his teachings **"the same Sun that melts the wax is the same Sun that hardens the clay"**. Both the wax and the clay come under the same heat of the Sun but the result is different because one material has a better depth for resistance to the heat than the other.

> **For we dare not make ourselves of the number, or compare ourselves with some that commend themselves: but they measuring themselves by themselves, and comparing themselves among themselves, are not wise.**
> **- 2nd Corinthians 10: 12 (KJV)**

Another reason why it is unwise to compare yourself with anyone is because you might as well be comparing your planting season to the harvesting season of another person. Be mindful of your timing.

Stay Rooted in God

As a child of God, it is important to understand where your strength comes from. Staying rooted in God is essential for growth and survival. When you experience growth, it should not be used as an excuse to abandon the very reason or source of your growth. An example of someone in the scripture that stayed true to his root is Isaac. Isaac stayed rooted and connected to the covenant God made with his Father, Abraham. God appeared to Isaac and instructed him:

> **"Do not go down to Egypt; live in the Land where I will tell you to live. Stay in this land for a while, and I will be with you and will bless you. For to you and your descendants I will give all these lands and will confirm the oath I swore to your father Abraham."**
> **- Genesis 26: 2-3 (NIV).**

The beginning of Genesis 26 tells us there was famine in the land, and it was usual for people to move from place to place in search of greener pastures. Even in today's world, it is not uncommon for people to flee economic hardship to other countries in search of a better life. Other people fled the land, when Isaac contemplated doing so but God instructed him to stay put in that land. I am sure in the eyes of others who had no relationship with God, it made no sense to remain in a land devastated by famine when others had fled for their lives. I can imagine people questioning Isaac's decision and calling him names. However, Isaac was rooted in God, so to obey God in that instance was not grievous to him.

While studying this passage, I stopped to think of how many times we have heard God's instruction on a matter but backed out because it doesn't go down well with us. How many times have we backed out of God's instruction because we had some information that seems to suggest that doing the contrary would produce a better result? Take the scriptural injunction that husbands should love their wives as Christ loves the church; many husbands are not living up to that bidding. And what we find are dysfunctional homes and marriages in the society. I recall travelling to the wedding ceremony of a Christian brother and coincidentally I sat beside a man on the train who was heading to the same event. We immediately clicked and started having a conversation about the intending couples and about marriage in general. He asked about my marital status and I informed him I wasn't married. Midway into our conversation, he began advising me about choosing a life partner and he said: "it is better

a woman loves her husband more than the husband loves her". I asked why and he told me that
from his experience, and from what he observed
in his environment, when a man loves his wife
more than the wife loves him, she would take him
for granted and the marriage would not work. He
continued: "but when the woman loves the man
more, the marriage is better positioned to work".
He went ahead to share his personal experience
with me and concluded that his first marriage
failed because he loved his wife more than she
loved him, but the peace he enjoys in his second
marriage is because his wife loves him more than
he loves her. He added that in his previous marriage, he could be away from his family for three
days and his ex-wife would not give him a call or
check on him but in his current marriage, he can't
be away from home for more than an hour without his wife checking on him. As if it was a con-
firmation, as he was still speaking, the wife called
him and after taking the call, he looked at me with
a grin on his face and said "I told you, she just
called to check on me". While I sympathise with
him for whatever he went through in his previous
marriage, there are so many things wrong with
the mentality he expressed towards marriage. I
do not know the totality or details of what went
wrong in his previous marriage but I am not entirely convinced it did not work because 'he loved

his wife more than she loved him'. As I kept thinking to myself, I wondered how philosophies such as the one the man enunciated towards marriage are gaining grounds against everything the scripture teaches on marriage such as **"Husbands, love your wives as Christ loved the church and gave himself for her" (Ephesians 5: 25).** The love Christ has for the church is not dependent on ours for Him. Rather, it is unconditional. It dawned on me that this is how we abandon godly instructions to adopt philosophies of men because society tells us godly instructions are too lofty to attain or are not ideal. How many times do we water down or minimise godly instructions because our personal experiences seem to contradict them? Isaac had enough experience as a farmer to know that famine was a dire situation and the land was unfruitful but that did not deter him from obeying God's instruction.

While the economic outlook for that climate was gloomy and there was no solution in sight, God instructed Isaac to remain there. How many times have we been swayed by popular opinion to a point where we think God's instruction does not count? How many times have we tried to modify God's instructions to us because they do not fit into societal standards or expectations? God's instruction to Isaac was backed with the promise of His blessing and His presence. How many times have we given up or backed out of God's instruction because it appeared His promise had not become our reality? What most of us will do today if we were in Isaac's shoes is to go back to God maybe we did not really hear Him or perhaps He would change His mind. We tend to assume the worst because of what we see around us and we sometimes keep seeking answers even after we have clearly heard God because what we heard doesn't sound favourable or possible in our limited understanding. God's instruction and promise to Isaac did not seem to tally with the reality on ground. It would have been challenging for him to imagine how there was going to be bumper harvests from a barren land. Despite all odds, he trusted God and remained confident in His promise.

> But blessed is the one who trusts in the Lord, whose confidence is in him. [8] They will be like a tree planted by the water that sends out its roots by the stream. It does not fear when heat comes; its leaves are always green. It has

no worries in a year of drought
and never fails to bear fruit.
– Jeremiah 17: 7 - 8 (NIV)

When we trust God and stay rooted in Him, we have no fear about how unpleasant the climate and our situation might be. The fact that we are connected to our roots gives us the assurance that even in the year of drought, we would bear fruits. This reminds me of one of my late mother's favourite hymns:

In times like these you need a Savior,
In times like these you need an anchor;
Be very sure, be very sure,
Your anchor holds and grips the Solid Rock!
This Rock is Jesus, Yes He's the One,
This Rock is Jesus, the only One;
Be very sure, be very sure,
Your anchor holds and grips the Solid Rock!

In times of drought, in times of famine, in times of uncertainty and in times of despair, if there's anything you must look out for, be sure you are anchored to God. He is our foundation and solid rock. When we are anchored to Him or rooted in Him, we will not be shaken. Even if we are swayed by the waves of the sea, we cannot drown. For Isaac to remain in the land, he also had to keep sowing even when it did not make sense to sow. It was one thing to be obedient and remain in the unproductive land and yet another to sow in the same land. Isaac understood the essence of complete obedience to the will of God. He did not only remain in the land, he sowed in the land as though everything was normal. The lesson here is that when God instructs us to wait on Him, we should continue doing what He expects from us in spite of the times.

> *#Complete obedience to God comes with a promise of His blessing and His presence.*

> **Isaac planted crops in that land and the same year reaped a hundredfold, because the LORD blessed him.**
> **– Genesis 26: 12 (NIV).**

I have dwelt on this story this much because most times that it is considered, verse 12 is usually the highlight how Isaac sowed in the time of famine and reaped a hundredfold in the same year followed by the submission that God's covenant with Abraham was responsible for Isaac's blessing at the time. True as it may be, we sometimes tend to forget that Isaac had his own part to play. The moment Isaac obeyed God's instruction, he 'activated' his harvests and 'oiled the lamp' of God's covenant with his father. It wasn't just sowing in famine that gave Isaac multiple harvests; it was his complete obedience to God that brought the harvests. Our obedience to God is truly tested when there is an opportunity to disobey God or when it doesn't 'make sense' to the human mind to obey God. Our obedience to God is truly tested when we experience famine in our finances, marital life and career and in other crucial areas of life. Isaac knew the planting conditions and the potency of his seeds weren't t just enough for great harvests but that staying rooted in God by obeying Him was equally vital. Isaac shows that when we stay rooted in God, we can experience harvests even when everything goes against us, when nothing is to our advantage and when the conditions are not perfect. We should understand that the moment we obey God even against popular opinion, we are in the majority. Even when we are in the minority, we are on the right track. To quote a popular cliché: "one with God is more than a majority". Isaac may have been tempted to leave the land because of the famine and because most people were leaving. He may have been burdened with the task of explaining to his family the rationale behind his decision to remain in the country at an austere time like that. Isaac may have second-guessed his decision; perhaps his family may not have been comfortable with his decision. But all those concerns did not stop him from obeying God and staying rooted in Him. Staying rooted in God will sustain us in famine, keep us through hard times and protect our seeds.

#*There is safety in obeying God*

A very typical example of someone that abandoned his root can be found in Luke 15: 11 - 32, popularly referred to as *the parable of the prodigal son*. In life, it is easy to be carried away by development and growth. The younger son probably thought he was of age and could manage his affairs hence he requested for his share of his father's property while his father was still alive. After the heat of the scourging sun descended on his seed, he squandered his resources because he lacked depth and was shallow minded. After friends who flocked around him for his wealth had deserted him, life hit him hard. Before long, it dawned on him that he still needed his father, his root.

Many people are always in a haste to disconnect themselves from their roots at the slightest seeming appearance of growth or progress. Some even become ashamed of their roots and do everything possible to severe their ties not wanting to identify any longer with that important part of their lives. Some may have acknowledged God as the source of their progress in the days of humble beginnings only to do everything later not to be seen as one who believes in God. It is a dangerous path to take in life. God remains the only reliable veritable source of growth and safety. It is suicidal therefore to cut yourself off from the very source that brought you to where you are. It's like a young child who flirts with the idea of leaving home to stay on his own without the parents. It's only a matter of time before he would realise he never paid bills or worked to eat while at home but would from that moment begin to fend for himself. It's only a matter of time he would understand the importance of safety and protection the parental home provided him.

> **And when he came to himself, he said, "How many hired servants of my father's have bread enough and to spare, and I perish with hunger! I will arise and go to my father, and will say unto him, Father, I have sinned against heaven, and before thee"- Luke 15:17-18 (KJV).**

"When he came to his senses" (NIV), he realized his mistakes and decided to reconnect with his root. There are times we need to evaluate our decisions and make amends where necessary. God has given us the power to think right. Sometimes what we need to triumph may not be any spiritual activity but a self-realization and a positive shift in our thought process. You would be shocked to know that many people never think through most decisions they make. They make decisions that would create dire consequences for them and their dependents without critical thinking. They become selfish and do not take into account the impact of their actions on others. It would have been better for the prodigal son to have come to his senses prior to embarking on such a destiny derailing journey. We tend to learn better from mistakes but it is still better to think through and avoid making such mistakes or at least learn from the mistakes of others because the consequence of mistake can be very expensive. The prodigal son came to his senses before he could get it right. This is a reminder that God has given us sound mind to make informed decisions. We have got to keep renewing it with the word of God. When we renew our minds with the word of God, it reminds us that God is our root and our source. When we begin to harbour selfish thoughts, it encourages us to be detached from our roots but renewing our minds with the word of God helps us recognize the source of our selfish thoughts and how to deal with them. Selfish thoughts make us forget there is a greater purpose for our seed of which many people are connected and should benefit from. When we renew our minds with the word of God, we are constantly reminded that our seeds are not just about us but about God's purpose and will, both for us and for humanity as a whole. When we re-new our minds with the word of God, it helps us weed out negative and defeating thoughts. When we renew our minds with the word of God, our negative thoughts are constantly redirected to the promises of God for our seeds and our lives. It is sometimes shocking how people constantly put themselves down with their thoughts. We have all been there at some point in our lives. If such moments are not properly handled, it could de-generate into confusion. Every time you think of a thousand and one reasons you would fail or why something might go sour, think of two thousand and one reasons why you could or must succeed. Use the sound mind God has given you to reset yourself into a positive posture as you stay rooted in Him.

#Thinking positively is not denying the unpleasant circumstances around you

*but it is denying those circumstances a
permanent place in your life.*

Jesus made a very profound statement in the
book of John:

**I am the vine, ye are the branch-
es: He that abideth in me, and I
in him, the same bringeth forth
much fruit: for without me ye can
do nothing – John 15: 5 (KJV)**

Always appreciate the fact that without Him
you can do nothing. Never contemplate breaking away from the vine because the consequences could be calamitous. No matter how big the
branch becomes, it can never survive without
the mother tree which is rooted in the soil. We
should be humble enough to realise we cannot be
bigger than our source. The vine is the source of
life for the branches without which the branches
will never bear fruit. Do you want to remain relevant at what you do? Do you want to experience
fulfilment with the seeds God has embedded in
you? Keep yourself plugged to the vine and you
would be guaranteed fruits and multiple seeds.
As believers, we are meant to bear good fruits.
Bearing good fruits is in our nature. The true test
and proof of our fellowship and oneness in God

is by the kind of fruits we bear. How I know that
I remain connected to the vine is by the fruits I
bear. These are some fruits you should look out
for in your life:

> **But the fruit of the Spirit is love,
> joy, peace, longsuffering, gentle-
> ness, goodness, faith, meekness,
> temperance: against such there
> is no law.**
> **– Galatians 5: 22 – 23 (KJV)**

*#God is the source and not the resource,
stay rooted in Him.*

Many of us think of God as our resource rather
than the source of all that we ever needed in life.
We think of God as a means to an end thus being fixated on only earthly benefits. We only stay
rooted in Him because of what we believe we can
get from Him. If the reason for staying rooted in
God is solely because of what a person stands to
gain in this life, the person could easily be swayed
if and when he can achieve his dreams and goals
when his commitment to God is not total.

Babies and toddlers cling to their parents ma-
jorly because of what they are getting from them.
They love the gifts the parents lavish on them.
Their focus is on those gifts not necessarily on the

parents because their brains are not developed enough to value their parents more than what they are getting from them. That perhaps may account for why people kidnap children with things as insignificant as sweets or cookies. But as you become a teenager and subsequently an adult, you appreciate your parents more for how they have been instrumental to your upbringing their limitations notwithstanding. Then, even when they can't provide all your needs or wants, you would still love them because all your life they have been there for you. It would be strange if as an adult, you decide to adopt 'new parents' solely because your biological parents couldn't meet some of your needs. If that happens, the person would not be different from a child who goes home with a stranger for giving him sweets or chocolates. As a parent, how would you feel if a child you did all your best for decides to abandon you because of what you could not afford for him? This mirrors how many people treat God. We behave like babies or toddlers when we should have become adults (with better understanding) if the sole reason for pitching tents with God is for selfish reasons. Even in human relationships, it is wrong to enter into relationship solely on the basis of what you stand to gain. You definitely wouldn't find it funny that the person you are committed to is after what he or she can extract from you.

For instance, while hunting for job, you are not likely to be hired if your prospective employer perceives that you are just desperate to eke a living without being prepared to contribute meaningfully to the overall wellbeing of the organisation. It is obvious everyone works to earn a living, but it would be absurd enlisting someone to work for you just because you want to take care of his financial needs. Naturally, if you are serious and passionate about your business or organisation, you will have to look out for virtues from your prospective hire such as competence, principles, values and interest in your brands.

I firmly believe that being rooted in God shouldn't be based merely on what we stand to gain from Him. Remember your seed is not just about you, it's about the bigger picture of God's plan for mankind through you. It's about God's masterplan. Therefore, cultivate your soil, increase your depth and stay rooted in God who is and should remain your source even when it appears all is not well.

CHAPTER 6

CHOKED BY THORNS

Other seed fell among thorns, which grew up and choked the plants, so that they did not bear grain. Mark 4: 7 (NIV)

SOME SEEDS FELL AMONG thorns; the soil seems right with enough nutrients and sufficient sunlight. Everything the seeds needed to grow was in place; so they germinated but never got to bear fruits. As the plants were growing, something else called thorns, which were detrimental to their growth, grew alongside with them. By nature, thorns are sharp pointed woody projections on the stem or other parts of a plant. They could prick or break human skin. Farmers don't joke with them; they are cut off as they spring up.

Characteristically, thorns are very unpleasant, discomforting to humans yet they can survive harsh environmental conditions.

So, the plants that grew among the thorns could not bear fruits because they were choked to death. They did not give enough allowance for the plants to grow optimally. Thorns also compete for soil nutrients with plants. It became difficult therefore for plants deprived of space and nutrients to grow, mature and bear fruits. When thorns are overgrown, they take over the land preventing sunlight from reaching the ground thereby killing other plants that are under them.

Every seed needs the best environment to flourish and produce fruits. You cannot surround yourself with thorns and expect to be fruitful. You cannot deliberately plant your seed in the midst of thorns and expect harvest. Thorns could mean people or anything including your immediate environment that would never give chance to your seeds. They are there to sap the strength you have and hurt you in the process. Have you ever been around certain people or places and you discover you cannot be productive? Are you always around people that emit negative energy? Are you always with people who have a pessimistic approach to everything? Are you around people who always focus on the worst-case scenario or outcome about anything? Are you around people that have the habit of killing your ideas before inception? Are you with people who constantly remind you of your weakness or failures?

Thorns stick around you only for what they can gain from you; they have no regards for your dreams and visions. If they show interest, it is because they are envisaging some gains from your seed. Thorns could be the bad habit you have developed over the years. It is important to know that you must be ready to give your all and take every necessary step for your seed to yield fruits. Avoid places, people and habits that consciously and unconsciously prevent you from optimizing the resources you have for your seed. I remember telling someone about writing and publishing to encourage believers. His advice was that I should keep writing but I should only publish when I have the platform to be heard (whatever that means). When I write, I imagine the finished product, with the cover illustration; I imagine people reading and being blessed. This in a way motivates me to continue. Why am I supposed to keep writing without thinking of publishing anytime soon? The mere thought of this began to discourage me because I thought I won't be read until I first had a platform to be heard. Each time I had the urge to write and I remember those words, I become demotivated to continue. This advice grew so fast in my thoughts to a point it slowed down my writing. Anyone who is experienced at farming or gardening will tell you weeds grow easier and sometimes faster than the useful plant. It is interesting to note that no matter how much you cultivate and prepare your soil for planting, weeds and thorns can do excellently well on your soil without any input from you. In the same vein, it doesn't take time for an unsolicited negative advice to kill your seeds. Just a little opinion or snide remarks are enough to make someone abandon the garden of his dream. I consciously flipped this thought that was brewing in my mind and told myself "my writing will provide the platform for me to be heard". I am sure this advice came with good intension but it was 'thorny' enough to kill my momentum. Thorns may come to you as people you regard and hold in high esteem. They may be close to you; they could be family members, friends, boss or even your spiritual leaders. Thorns may not necessarily be out to choke life out of your plant, they could be well-meaning but you must be able to discern when they are counterproductive to your seed.

Jesus Christ said "get thee behind me Satan" after Peter rebuked Him when He revealed His purpose and mission on earth. Peter was looking up to Jesus so he could not come to terms with the prospect of Jesus being killed. But Jesus understood the purpose for which He came and which

He had to fulfil. No thorn in the form of a close associate like Peter was convincing enough to discourage Him (Matthew 16: 21 - 23). Whatever takes away strength from the life of your plant must not be pampered. Whoever or whatever chokes life out of your visions, dreams, goals or purpose must not be tolerated. When you allow thorns in your garden, they will certainly choke life out of your plants. If the plants survive they will not bear fruits and if they bear fruits, they will be substandard. Thorns want you to do fine but not good enough to experience a major breakthrough in your academics, career, calling or pursuit. They are okay with you as long as you will not bear fruits. They will allow you to grow as long as you will not outshine them. Thorns want to pull you back and keep you stuck in the same spot. You have to understand that thorns will never bear fruits or at best, they bear unwanted fruits. Their aim therefore is for you not to bear appreciable fruits. Thorns want to restrict you. They are happy with your success as long as it doesn't trump theirs. Sometimes weeds or thorns are subtle, they could look exactly like the real plant thereby making it difficult for you to differentiate the cultivated from the uncultivated. There are friends who would like to remind you of some nasty experiences they or others may have had whenever you try to share your good plans with them rather than rejoice and be happy with you. They want your attention and everything about you to be centred around them. They consciously or unconsciously try to link everything good that must have happened to you to their benevolence or goodwill to you. Sometimes they'll make bold claims that their mere presence in your life is the reason for your growth (true or not, they use it as a form of manipulation to keep you perpetually subservient to them). Whenever you come up with an idea, they come up with a counter idea to kill your idea so that they can become the focal point. It takes divine wisdom to see through such people because they do it with so much wit and charm.

Fear – thorn seed
Earlier in Chapter 2 we talked about trusting God and not allowing fear to prevent us from beginning our seed sowing project. Even after we have sown our seeds, fear could still creep in like a thorn to destroy our labour. Here is a note about the seed of fear from Stephanie Thomas:

> *This seed destroys the good seeds. It's a powerful poisonous seed with the ability to whither everything it can reach for- it consumes like a hungry lion. Its best friend is destruc-*

tion. But let me clarify, it doesn't necessarily immediately destroy the things around you, but it destroys the one thing you need to maintain all that you have built and to keep on building. That one thing, my friend, is faith. As Christians we are powerless without faith. Apostle Paul sternly wrote in Hebrews the following: "without faith it is impossible to please the Lord...." (Heb 11:6) Impossible! There is no way you can glorify God without faith. God cannot cause His face to shine upon you without faith. You cannot lift your hands up in confidence while praying without faith. Forget the possibility of coming to ask God for anything before His throne without faith. "Let us then with confidence draw near to the throne of grace, that we may receive mercy and find grace to help in time of need" (Hebrews 4:16). I hope you can now see the gravity of the seed of fear. It destroys, it kills, it takes away that which is good. It's the devil's greatest weapon. If he gets you to believe his lies he can paralyze you to the point of absolute inactivity- all because he succeeded in making False Evidence Appear Real. Well, we can now focus on how to pluck out the seed of fear before it starts to kill the other seeds in the garden of our hearts. Believe it or not dear reader, it's a simple two-step process.

A dear ex-colleague of mine opened my heart to understanding this:

Step 1: Imagine the worst thing that could possibly happen in your current situation; this captures your biggest fear. If you stop at this point, paralysis takes place. The scenario you imagine starts to transform into a reality in your heart. While this takes place, all other good seeds are destroyed, and faith disappears. However, I implore you not to stop here; move on to step two.

Step 2: Now, imagine that it really happens. I guess you weren't expecting me to say that! But let me go further. Imagine that it really happens, but also, while you imagine this scenario, imagine God giving you all the grace you need during that situation to carry you through. The worst-case scenario is not something to fear because the God you serve will give you all the help that you need through that period. He already knows what you need if that thing were to ever happen!

144

I hope you can now see why fear is not worth your time. The fact that it kills faith is enough reason not to engage in entertaining this seed. Those without Christ can't move to step two. I will however say that there are people without Christ who actually understand the principle of step two better than many Christians in that they consciously decide not to worry about tomorrow and if their worst fear becomes reality, they will be positive about it and do their best to keep on living life. But we Christians have something better than 'positive thinking' and doing our best. We have Almighty God! The Sovereign God of the universe is right by our side! How can we lose sight of this and remain paralyzed at step one? Let that not be said of us! Let the seed of faith kill the seed of fear. Your faith must lie in who God is. You must know the God you pray to. You must believe what He has said in His word, you must remember the times He gave you grace during the difficult seasons of your life. The God who parted the Red sea is just the same today. He parted the Red sea over 3300 years ago. What potential Red sea would He not be able to part in your life? Now, if He is able, why fear that you would drown in that Red sea. As a child of God your story will not end like that of the Egyptians, it will follow the pattern of the Israelites; they crossed the Red Sea on DRY LAND. Our God is awesome, let this faith kill fear.

*The Hymn below by Eliza E. Hewitt captures what I
have just explained:*

> The God who led His people thro'
> the parted sea,
> And from Egyptian bondage, set
> His children free,
> Who rain'd down bread from
> heaven all the pilgrim way,
> Is the God to whom I pray.
> Just the same today, just the same
> today,
> As when He led His people thro' the
> sea;
> His trustful child I'll be,
> For in His word I see,
> The God who doeth wonders
> Is just the same today

Deal with thorns before your plant becomes one

The major reason we sow seeds is to get fruits; a plant that does not bear fruit is useless, it is not different from weeds or thorns. A tree that is expected to produce fruit but doesn't is a waste of resources such as time and labour. No one will be willing to invest in anything that will yield no result. The first step in dealing with thorns is to identify them and recognize how they can damage seeds. If you do not identify thorns in your life or you cannot tell how exactly they can negatively affect your seeds, it will be impossible to effectively deal with them. The fact that thorns could be a habit, something or someone really close to you can make them difficult to identify. But if you are on a conscious seed sowing mission, it won't take long before they begin to differ from every other plant in the garden of your life. For instance, there may be habits or routines you have imbibed that are not in themselves bad or harmful but which in the long run could take too much of your resources. They are thorns to your plants. Sometimes, everyone else can see how they constitute thorns in your garden but you can't. It is a daunting task to stop someone from doing something he doesn't see as bad or how it is impacting his life negatively. How do you convince a workaholic to slow down or have some break? You can clearly see how his work is taking a toll on his health physically and mentally but he may not be able to see it. No matter how you try, until he can see and understand the need to rest, your effort at helping him may be in vain.

Identifying thorns is a step you have to take on your own. There's a limit to how far anyone can help you identify or deal with thorns choking out life from your plants. You have the full autonomy to cultivate the garden of your life and give account to God who provided you with the seeds. Therefore, take full responsibility for how you handle your plants.

> **And now also the axe is laid unto the root of the trees: therefore every tree which bringeth not forth good fruit is hewn down, and cast into the fire.**
> **– Matthew 3: 10(KJV)**

A tree that does not bear fruit is regarded as an unwanted plant. It is good for nothing and so must be cut down and cast into the fire. When you identify thorns cut them off. Your plant is not different from thorns if they do not bear fruit and to avoid your plant becoming like a thorn, you have to do something about the thorns as fast as you can. Do you know how farmers treat weeds and thorns? Have you seen how a land that has been abandoned with overgrown weeds is treated? They become a dumping ground for all manner of things but when the land is ready to be cultivated or used, everything on it is levelled to the ground. In dealing with thorns you have to be careful, decisive and sometimes brutal without apologies. This could mean assessing your growth and doing away with whatever constitutes a thorn to your seeds. Make an assessment of the people in your life and how much they contribute to the growth of your seed or otherwise. If they are like thorns to your seed, cut them off or at the very least, limit their influence on your plant. This might sound harsh or too direct but it's the only way to effectively deal with thorns because the longer you allow them with your plants, the more harm they do to them and subsequently to your harvests. Uproot them from the garden of your life before your plants become unfruitful like them.

Many shy away from confronting thorns and taking the decisive step of cutting them off; they pamper and try to ease them out with some mild approach probably to be likeable or not to offend anyone. Your seeds or your plants have a time-line and when you do not deal with thorns at the right time, it might be impossible to benefit from your labour when the time for harvests comes. If you did not deal with certain habits at a certain period in your life, it may be almost impossible to stop them when they begin to negatively affect the productive areas of your life. If you entertain or accommodate certain people who choke life out of your seed, when they finally leave it might be too late to begin sowing your seeds again especially when it's past the sowing season of your life. God has given every one of us time for our seeds, a time for planting and a time for harvest. Our seeds sowing engagement and harvests are restricted to a particular time. No one will be on earth for ever and no one can determine how long he would live.

A person's days are determined; you have decreed the number of his months and have set limits he cannot exceed. - Job 14: 5(NIV)

Thorns will attempt to steal your time because when you lose your time, your seeds become impotent. You may successfully obtain a bachelor's degree with distinctions at 80 years of age but it is most likely not going to be useful to you again. At best you will make the headlines news for having obtained a Bachelor's degree at 80. A limit is set to our days on earth. Unfortunately, because it appears we have a lot of time, we rarely take our time seriously. Consequently, we allow thorns to engage us in frivolous activities. Time waits for no one and it is no respecter of persons. Whether you are aware of your time or not, when it is gone, it is gone. The only question you will need to answer is how you spent it. But before long, time itself will reveal to the world how you spent yours. Because of the understanding of time and its limitedness, employers of labour determine the pay check of their employees according to the value of time they put into work and governments set minimum wages according to what they consider the appropriate value of time in their territory or economy. Every second of one's life counts. If anyone successfully steals the seconds of a person's time, essentially the days of the person life has been stolen. You will not find any successful farmer out there who doesn't respect time and season. In the same vein, when we cultivate our seeds, we must do so having the consciousness of our limitations in time. We must also learn to aggressively fight thorns that are out to steal or waste the time of our precious seeds.

> *#Your seed or your plant has a timeline and when you do not deal with thorns at the right time, it might be impossible to benefit from your seed when it is time for harvest.*

When farmers are working on the farm and performing task such as weeding, they wear personal protective equipment (PPE) such as hard hats, gloves (i.e. cactus gloves), safety glasses, and latex/rubber footwear for protection. Thorns or prickly weeds could be dangerous or poisonous and when they come in contact with the human body they could cause infection, serious illness or even death. When dealing with thorns, be sure to take protective measures so you are not harmed or destroyed in the process. For instance, the fact that you should cut off or reduce the influence certain people (who do not favour your seed sowing mission) have on you does not mean you shouldn't do it with tact and wisdom, especially if they are close to you. As mentioned earlier, some are not deliberately out to kill your plant; they may mean well for you. This reminds me of how Joseph planned to divorce Mary when he discovered she was pregnant. Though Mary was betrothed to him, they had not lived as husband and wife and so Joseph thought she must have been pregnant for another man. **"Because Joseph her husband was faithful to the law, and yet did not want to expose her to public disgrace, he had in mind to divorce her quietly – Matthew 1: 19 (NIV).** Joseph planned to cut Mary off from his life because he believed she had suddenly become unsuitable for him as wife. He planned to divorce her quietly so it wouldn't bring her shame or humiliation. On the flip side, I also do not see how this would have brought a positive publicity or image for Joseph if he decided to put her away in a loud and brash manner. My point is that cutting her off with tact and wisdom was best for her and for him also. Thankfully, an angel visited him in his dream to inform him that the baby Mary was carrying was not conceived by human but through the Holy Spirit. As you cut off thorns, be practical and tactical on how you go about it. More importantly, seek divine wisdom; God is able to direct you.

An interesting fact about weeds in the farm is that sometimes you can't get rid of them completely. They tend to grow again after some time therefore you have to be vigilant to control them. Some thorns or weeds can't be totally eliminated from the garden of your life. Sometimes God allows them to keep you constantly on your toes. At other times God will "prepare a table for you in the presence of your enemies". In other words, not every enemy of your life will be destroyed before you grow your seed. Such thorns allowed by God will have to be monitored and controlled consistently. Cases in point are some habits you may not be able to totally eliminate from your life but which can be brought under control. Maybe you were born in a country or live in an environment that negatively impacts your life. You may not be able to totally eliminate the negative influence of such an environment from your life and family but you can significantly reduce their impacts on your life and on your outlook to life. There are people who were born into a very disadvantaged environment but have chosen not to allow the influence of such an environment impact their lives or their seeds negatively. Martin Luther, the fifteenth century German professor of theology said; **"You cannot keep birds from flying over your head but you can keep them from building a nest in your hair"**. There are thorns you can't stop from growing in the garden of your life, but you can prevent them from choking your plants. You need to consistently monitor your garden and uproot these thorns and weeds from time to time before they are powerful enough to impact your plants. This is hard work which takes a lot of effort but no effort is too much to invest in caring for the plants in the garden of your life. You may also replace thorns and weeds with seeds; this is another means of reducing their influence. Reliance on God's promises and acting according to His direction go a long way in helping us to uproot thorns and weeds from our lives. This is not easy; it is only through the grace of God that we can find strength to keep weeding until it becomes part of us and then a habit with a meaning.

> Jesus told them another parable: "The kingdom of heaven is like a man who sowed good seed in his field.[25] But while everyone was sleeping, his enemy came and sowed weeds among the

wheat, and went away.[26] When the wheat sprouted and formed heads, then the weeds also appeared.[27] "The owner's servants came to him and said, 'Sir, didn't you sow good seed in your field? Where then did the weeds come from?' Matthew 13: 24 - 27(NIV)

There is a need to watch and pray always because the devil walks to and fro looking for good seeds to devour. The devil is not after your seeds because of you but because of their divine origin and the expected harvests. God invested in you because of those your fruits are meant to feed. Trust the devil to truncate those divine agenda if you are careless about them. He waits for the most vulnerable moments so that he can strike. Jesus alerted us to be aware of satanic agenda to sow weeds among the wheat when we sleep. We all sleep at night, including plants and animals. The night is a time of rest for most living things on earth. Unfortunately, it is the most preferred period for evil entities to perpetuate their wickedness since the night provides cover for them. The psalmist calls it **"the terror by night and the pestilence that stalks in the darkness"** Psalm 91: 5 - 6 (NIV). The terror by night and the pestilence that stalks in darkness can also happen in the day, but the cover of the dark makes them more effective or lethal at night because typically there is low vision at night. In essence, the night is a period of vulnerability. When we sleep we lose consciousness of our environment.

We may be found asleep at different periods in our lives' journey. This could be the period when progress in our lives appear slow, when we are demotivated, when our thoughts become cloudy, when our vision for the future becomes blurry, when we are consumed by fear, when we are disappointed and fixated on our failures and shortcomings and sometimes too busy looking at the past, while failing to see the future. This is when the enemy comes to strike and pollute the garden of lives with thorns. Never be caught sleeping when you should be awake. Don't give the devil any chance to sow weeds in your garden. Work on your dreams. Your dream is not what you experience when you sleep rather it is what doesn't allow you to sleep. Never lose consciousness of your dreams, goals, vision, values and purpose. The reason for your scarcity, lack and want may be because of your sleep. There is no room for sleep, not even a nap. When you sleep a little, weeds and thorns outgrow your plants. When it's time for harvest you would have no fruits. Until you begin to dream and discover your precious seeds and decide to grow them, you would always find yourself asleep. Seed discovery and planting is a process that requires being alert spiritually and physically. You must understand God is the only help you need to fight the enemy that is waiting for you to fall asleep in order to pollute your garden with thorns.

**Watch and pray so that you will not fall into temptation. The spirit is willing, but the flesh is weak.
- Matthew 26: 41 (NIV)**

The need to combine watching with prayers is because we are human; our flesh is weak and will always fail. Prayer therefore is the only guarantee to strength in times of weakness. Prayer energizes the spirit. Even when the flesh is weak, your energised spirit will keep you going when you pray.

#The fastest route to poverty, lack and scarcity is to take a nap when you should be planting.

Prayer cannot be overemphasized in our seed sowing exercise. When we pray, we admit our strength is not enough and we lean on the strength and grace of our heavenly Father to conquer.

CHAPTER 7

GROWTH AND HARVEST

Still other seed fell on good soil. It came up, grew and produced a crop, some multiplying thirty, some sixty, some a hundred times." Mark 4: 8 (NIV)

IN THIS PARABLE OF the sower that we have been looking at, the soil played a very important role in the growth of the seed as we have seen. Some seeds fell on a fertile soil (resource). The environment was right, thorns were absent and the seeds sprouted, grew and produced plants that yielded good fruits as was expected. The

159

seeds needed not just a resource but a good resource (fertile soil). The success of these set of seeds had much to do with the soil they were planted in. Other seeds that did not yield fruits were as good as these set of seeds but could not do well because of where they were planted. This clearly shows that it is not every soil that is good for planting. In other words, not every resource is good for our seeds. It is not everything that appears useful to others that are bound to work for you. Every seed needs different kind of environment or soil to flourish. It is your responsibility to understand your soil to know whether or not it will be suitable for your seeds. My walk with God has taught me that not everything that works for others will work for me. The tools and the resources you use have to be good enough for your seed. There's an adage that says: **"A man is only as good as his tools"**.

Growth

For your seed to yield the desired result, growth is inevitable. This is an aspect in our seed sowing-growing mission where we need to be sensitive to the fact that besides our effort, God is an indispensable factor.

> **I planted the seed, Apollos watered it, but God has been mak-**

ing it grow.[7] So neither the one who plants nor the one who waters is anything, but only God, who makes things grow – 1st Corinthians 3: 6 - 7 (NIV)

In the context of this passage, Paul was speaking about his labour and that of Apollos in the establishment of the Church at Corinth while at the same time emphasising the God factor in the growth process that they recorded. We should always have it at the back of our minds that irrespective of the effort we put into our seed sowing enterprise, it is God's prerogative to engender growth. God is the life of our seeds and without life in them, they are dead. Many of us take pride in our work and so we put in so much effort. When our efforts yield results, we beat our chests believing we were solely responsible. Yes, you planted and watered but God gave the growth. For every opportunity or success you can boast of, I can show you ten people who probably put in more effort than you did without any tangible results. Whenever you are tempted to be puffed up by your achievements or when people intentionally or unintentionally make your head to swell up in pride, remind yourself that it was God that gave you the growth. No work can prosper without Him. He is the one that blesses the works of our hands. Our skills, labour, expertise and knowledge would all be in vain if God does not bless them. I know there are scientific explanations for how seeds grow when they are planted; there are explanations for how elements in the soil affect seeds and how the nutrients in the soil make seeds produce fruits. We know of so many principles and guidelines on how to make good use of the gifts God has given us, but do not forget that all the elements and planting conditions may be right and yet some seeds would not produce good fruits. You can follow all the rules in the book but achieve no tangible results. We have to come to the point of realising that nothing is really worth the trouble if God is not in it (Ecclesiastes 11:5). So learn to always give God the credit.

> **Unless the Lord builds the house, the builders labour in vain, Unless the Lord watches over the city, the guards stand watch in vain – Psalm 127:1 (NIV)**

The builders can build all they like and in one second fire or earthquake can reduce it to rubbles. Remember what happened to the tower of Babel; it wasn't completed because God was not in support of the idea (Genesis 11: 1 – 9). Men have researched, toiled and worked night and day into erecting structures and embarking on huge projects that never saw the light of day. Our safety and security is not assured because we are cautious about how we live our lives or because the law enforcement agencies are capable of protecting everybody every time but because God is in the business of securing us. We will never know how close we have been to danger but came out unscathed. We will never know how many times we walked through the valley of the shadow of death without a scratch. The point here is simple, we have to learn to take a step backward in victory or defeat in our seed sowing effort and acknowledge the sovereignty of God. When we learn to acknowledge and accept the sovereignty of God in our lives, we put ourselves in a position where we can be more receptive to His will and direction for our lives. When we open our hearts to receive of His will, we give room for growth in our lives. If and when we expect our seeds to grow and it doesn't happen the way we expected, we should not be tempted to stay focused on the bad outcome and conclude that all is lost. Why? There are lessons we are bound to learn in such circumstances that will turn out to be profitable. We often fail to realise that failure itself is part of growth. Growth is continuous and it is a process that will continue until we leave the earth.

I have learnt to see my failures and defeats as part of my growth process while still trusting God to relaunch. As you trust God, learn to pick out the positives in the process and rejoice over them. Don't just be joyful because you have to be joyful but "enjoy your joyfulness". In fact, this book you are reading was borne out of a hunger and search for answers in my gloomy moments, when the future looked bleak, uncertain and cloudy. It was in the search for answers that I received a different insight and meaning into why I needed to go back to the drawing board and look at my life as a destined seed.

Enjoy your Harvest
While sharing with you my lessons about growth and harvest, I must confess that I struggled to bring myself to fully understand that it is God's will for us to enjoy the harvest from our seeds. Let me crave your indulgence to say that in God's grand scheme of things, our seeds are not just about us but rather, they are beyond us. We are all here to act on the script written and directed by the Master. Many Christians are of the opinion that enjoying our lives on earth is contrary to the teachings of the Holy Scriptures. But as we look at the totality of the Scriptures as touching God's will for us, we continually see that we are

admonished to enjoy the myriad of provisions God has made available to us.

> **This is what I have observed to be good: that it is appropriate for a person to eat, to drink and to find satisfaction in their toilsome labour under the sun during the few days of life God has given them—for this is their lot.**[19] **Moreover, when God gives someone wealth and possessions, and the ability to enjoy them, to accept their lot and be happy in their toil—this is a gift of God.**
> **– Ecclesiastes 5: 18 - 19 (NIV)**

We can clearly see in the passage above that it is appropriate to be satisfied with whatever we have been able to gather in this world through honest means though the same Ecclesiastes describes all earthly possessions as vain and meaningless. When God gives us the strength to profit from our seeds, to make tangible harvests and to enjoy them, it is a gift from Him. This struck me so hard. In other words, it is possible to have a good harvest and not enjoy your harvest. It means when we have the opportunity to be joyful in our harvests, it is a gift and blessing from God.

More importantly, our satisfaction or pleasure is appropriate when it is God centred. Don't be like the rich fool in Luke 12: 16 – 21. All grace comes from God. There is nothing modest in shying away from taking absolute pleasure and satisfaction from your labour and your sweat. If you find it difficult to enjoy the harvest from your seeds, you might need to probe yourself. Every good and perfect gift comes from God (James 1: 17) without any unpleasant attachment and burden. In whatever field of endeavour you find yourself, you are allowed to enjoy and reap the rewards they bring to you. If you have sowed your seed(s), you deserve your harvests and you should not deny yourself the opportunity of enjoying them.

#The ability to enjoy your harvest is a Gift from God

Even as we derive pleasure and joy from our harvest, God expects our harvest to bring honour and glory to Him (Proverbs 3: 9). We can't be carried away deriving pleasure from our harvest in a way that dishonours the God who made it possible. We can't use our harvest to disobey God and gratify the longings of our flesh.

If they obey and serve him, they shall spend their days in prosper-

ity, and their years in pleasures.
- Job 36: 11 (KJV)

For some, the only way they know how to be joyful or enjoy whatever God has given them is to engage in sin. Even as we take delight in our harvests, the guarantee that we will continue to experience joy and pleasure all the days of our lives is hinged on our obedience to God. Don't let the good harvests God has given you lead you to the path where continuous joy departs from you because you are disobeying and dishonouring God while seeking pleasure due to your bumper harvests.

Multiply Your Seeds

Don't stop at harvesting the rewards of the seeds you sowed. Ensure you multiply those seeds in as many lives as possible. Your harvest is not only what you gain from your seed, your harvest is also how much seeds you have been able to create or how much of your seeds you have been able to multiply. One of the first commands that God gave to man can be found in Genesis 1: 28 (KJV):

> And God blessed them, and God
> said unto them, Be fruitful, and
> multiply, and replenish the earth,
> and subdue it: and have domin-

ion over the fish of the sea, and over the fowl of the air, and over every living thing that moveth upon the earth.

God expects every seed He has embedded in us to produce fruits. Your seeds and your harvest are tied to many destinies. When you do not produce fruits, you deprive those destinies substantially. In other words, the manifestation of your seed becomes a testimony and a spring board for others. God has blessed us with various gifts and talents in order to bless others. Our gifts enable others to begin their mission of sowing their own seeds. God is not just asking us to be fruitful but He commands us to multiply. To multiply means our seed should give birth to seeds in the lives of others. There is no reason you should be extremely good at something without teaching or mentoring others within the circle of your influence to become as good as you are or better than you. One reason for multiplication of seed is because we will not be on earth forever and there will always be a need for our seed. The world has come a long way technologically because man has always looked for ways to pass discovered and acquired knowledge down to the next generation. The world would be a step backward if early scientists died with their discoveries and research findings without passing them down to those who could improve upon them to solve present day challenges. We may take a look at the Council of the European Union which pushed for open access to EU funded research and data to have it fully achieved by 2020. This was a deliberate step towards giving more individuals access to information they need to proffer solutions to challenges in our world today. Societies and individuals that understand the need to multiply seeds are always at the top, because as seeds get multiplied they are also improved. Don't just bear fruits from your seeds but endeavour to multiply the seeds also.

Seed multiplication means impacting people directly and indirectly for them to discover their own seeds. This is a key to finding fulfilment. Your seed will only be multiplied after you have sown them and received your harvest. Therefore, seed multiplication is tied to your harvest. If I am a talented footballer seeking to start a professional football career and I am in need of a mentor, I will most likely look out for footballers around me who have achieved the most in their footballing career. This means I will only look for footballers who have visible and tangible harvest from their seeds. I will only trust those who have made good use of their seeds to help me harness mine. How much have you documented your journey and process for others coming after you? How much of your stories have you told others to inspire them? How many people have you brought under your wings or tutelage? How deliberate have you been in steering your children or those who look up to you through the path you once walked? I don't just mean dishing out moral instructions or conventional life lessons but actually looking at their journey in today's world through their eyes and equipping them for the challenges ahead while helping them navigate the challenges of today. This reminds me of Steve Irwin, host of the famed wildlife documentary television series titled *The Crocodile Hunter* which was aired from 1997 through 2004 with about 67 episodes. The Australian and his wife Terri ran a wildlife refuge and gave the world a peek into the animal kingdom in the most fascinating, educative and engaging manner on television. The conservationist and wildlife expert was especially skilled in handling reptiles, including dangerous crocodiles and venomous snakes. Anybody who knows a thing or two about wildlife will tell you Steve Irwin was so good at what he did and no one rivalled him. On the 4th of September 2006 while on a location in Queensland Australia filming a new underwater documentary series, Steve Irwin was stabbed by a stingray and was rushed to a medical facility where he was pronounced dead. The news of his death sent shock waves around the world; the man who appeared invincible handling some of the deadliest reptiles of this planet on television was gone. In 2018 it was inspiring and comforting to hear Steve's wife and their children Bindi and Robert announce a new television series about nature. They talked about continuing the work of their father and keeping his legacy. I kept wondering why they would want to continue dealing with dangerous animals, a job that killed their father. I dug deeper into this family and discovered Steve's father, was a globally recognized herpetologist. Steve's love for conservation and wildlife was passed down to him by his father and his children carried on from where he stopped. His death did not deny or stop the world from benefiting from their gifts. It is refreshing and inspiring whenever you listen to his children talk about him, his work and the work they have continued to do in caring and looking out for endangered animal species. In an interview on NBC's *Today Show* in 2018, Bindi made a statement that stayed with me, it was in reference to continuing their wildlife work; "I think it's a part of who we are and not just what we do" she said. When you see your seeds not just as what you do but as you, you will have a better understanding of why you should multiply those seeds in the lives of others God has placed within the sphere of your influence. Your seed is who you are. It was evident the work of Steve Irwin had not only impacted the world but also those in his closest sphere of influence: his family. Even though he died when Bindi and Robert were 8 and 2 respectively, they had enough influence from their father's work to carry it on. Start looking for ways to spur the growth of seeds in those God has placed directly under you; begin with your family and people who are in your life. We have an unparalleled example in Jesus Christ. He chose twelve men to be with Him because of the assignment of reconciling man to God. By the time He left the earth, he had deposited seeds of the gospel in the men such that they went out to spread the seeds of the gospel to the ends of the earth. The gospel would not have been here with us today if Jesus Christ had preached salvation, drew men to God and left the earth without making any deliberate effort to disciple men who would continue after Him.

#Don't just bear fruits, multiply your seeds in the lives of others.

Learn Contentment

But godliness with contentment is great gain – 1st Timothy 6: 6 (NIV)

As we experience growth and bountiful harvests from our seeds in different areas of life, we must also learn to embrace the virtue of contentment. Contentment is simply being appreciative and satisfied with what we have. When we are not contented, we are focused on what we do not have and we may begin to lose sight of what we have and where we are going. Contentment is not being lazy, unambitious and living life without goals or a purpose but rather it is living a life that trusts in the sufficiency of God to bring us to a better place in our seed sowing project without having to worry or get involved in murky waters. The world today appears to encourage dissatisfaction. There was a time in my life I thought going to college or university will bring me unlimited joy. I thought I would feel more established in life after earning my first pay check with my degree. Nothing changed much even after that because I still felt unsatisfied as I could see both current and future bills I would have to settle. It sometimes feels like a hole you are obliged to keep filling but which would never get filled. Most times what we think would bring us to that ultimate happiness and satisfaction is nothing but a mirage. Surprising though, nobody gives up searching for that El Dorado because our environment conditions us so to do. Everyone seems to contend with one form of discontent or the other. Contentment is a choice and we must be deliberate about being contented. Paul boldly proclaimed he had to learn to be contented both in times of plenty and in times of little (Philippians 4: 11 - 12). Being contented should not be determined by our current state or condition but on the sufficiency of our God. As we seek to maximize the potentials God has planted in us, and as we enjoy growth and harvest from time to time, we must constantly fix our gaze on God and absolutely trust in Him if we must be contented and grateful for our life's journey. Never forget that Christ is enough for you.

CONCLUSION

Then Jesus said, "Whoever has ears to hear, let them hear." Mark 4: 9 (NIV)

AFTER JESUS FINISHED NARRATING the parable of the sower, He ended with this touching warning in Mark 4: 9. We see Jesus using this expression often in the Scriptures to drive home His messages. Like here, He wanted special attention to be paid to the message because of its importance. Everyone may hear a message, but not everyone will consider it important. Some may consider it important but not all will take the required action of living the message. We should not just learn these lessons about our lives as seeds or the fact that God has planted some seeds inside us, but more importantly, we should begin to live it out in reality. If you paid close attention to what you have read so far, you would have observed one embedded theme in each of the verses of our study passage in Mark 4:1-9 which is 'a **call to take action now**'.

Every chapter in this book is a prompting for us to take action and begin to live the life God has destined for us. While writing down this piece to share with you, my aim was not just to motivate or inspire you but to encourage you to spring into action immediately and sow the seeds in your hands. The reason for this is because when we feel motivated or inspired only, it creates a hunger for us to begin work on our seeds but it may not sustain us through the journey especially when faced with obstacles and the initial excitement begins to wane. However, when we take concrete action with an end goal in sight, it fuels our motivation to keep pushing through as we move forward. In other words, don't just read this book and feel inspired, motivated or excited; take a step further by taking some tangible action now with the seeds in your hands. Your motivation will not take you to your goals but rather your actions will especially if you understand that your destiny has been divinely ordained and that God expects great harvests from your seeds. The harvests from your seeds are the right pieces

CONCLUSION

God needs to make the puzzles of life in your dispensation fit together. Beloved, rise and sow your seeds NOW!

CPSIA information can be obtained
at www.ICGtesting.com
Printed in the USA
LVHW110820190922
728707LV00001B/154